Philip Guston's
Late Work ▫

A MEMOIR

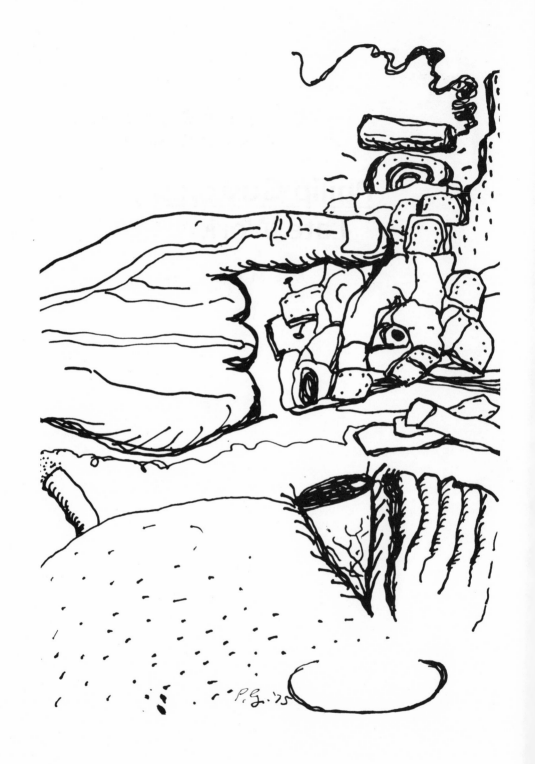

Philip Guston's Late Work:

A MEMOIR

by

William Corbett

Z

ZOLAND BOOKS

Cambridge, Massachusetts

First edition published in 1994 by
Zoland Books, Inc.
384 Huron Avenue
Cambridge, MA 02138

Excerpts from "East Coker" in *Four Quartets*, copyright 1943 by T.S. Eliot and renewed
1971 by Esme Valerie Eliot, reprinted by permission of Harcourt Brace & Company.

Library of Congress Cataloging-in-Publication Data

Corbett, William, 1942-
     Philip Guston's late work : a memoir / by William Corbett. — 1st ed.
     p. cm.
     Includes bibliographical references (p. 118).
     ISBN 0-944072-43-7
     1. Guston, Philip, 1913-1980 — Criticism and intrepretation.
     2. Guston, Philip, 1913-1980 — Friends and associates. 3. Corbett,
     William, 1942-   — Relations with artists. 4. Painters — United
     States — Biography. I. Guston, Philip, 1913-1980. II. Title.
ND237.G8C67   1994
759. 13 — dc20
[B]   94-14571
                                                                CIP

*This book is printed on acid-free paper,
and its binding materials have been chosen for strength and durability.*

Designed by Jeanne Abboud

10 9 8 7 6 5 4 3 2 1

Printed in the United States of America

For
Clark and Susan Coolidge
&
Charles and Helen Simic

Contents

Acknowledgments

This book leans on four books that came before it: Dore Ashton's *Yes, but . . .* , Ross Feld's *Philip Guston,* Robert Storr's *Philip Guston,* and Musa Mayer's *Night Studio.* Except for the Feld they are in print today and worth hunting up. During the years of my friendship with Guston I did not keep a diary. I remember the gist of our conversations, but rarely his exact words. Where my memory of what Guston said jibes with words recorded by Ashton, Feld, Storr, and Mayer I have quoted their versions, and I have also quoted Guston's public statements. Any and all errors and blind spots in this book are mine alone.

My thanks to Askold Melnyczuk of *Agni* and Joseph and Molly Torra of *lift,* Mark Salerno of *Arshile,* Michael Gizzi of *Lingo,* and Seth Frechie of *To.* These editors printed sections of this book, thereby encouraging me and letting me see what my words looked like in print.

Paul Auster, Jane Gunther, and Bill Berkson read this book in manuscript and gave excellent editorial advice. They made this a better book, and they have my gratitude.

Most importantly I thank my dear wife, Beverly Corbett, who listened to the spoken version of this book and read an early draft. She has an original eye, and some of her insights are here in my own words. I am a grateful husband.

Introduction

In 1980, after I wrote the poems that end this book, I had no thought of writing anything else about Philip Guston, much less a memoir. But as the fame of his late work grew, and his name came up, I talked about him at length. I greatly enjoyed remembering him in this way. Then I wrote a few casual essays about his work, and a more considered essay detailing how knowing him had influenced me as a writer.

In the course of things, Robert Storr interviewed my wife, Beverly, and me for his book on Philip. We talked all one Sunday afternoon and, while drinking more than one bottle of wine, into the night. Waking, hungover and ashamed, the morning after Storr's visit, I felt I had been completely untrue to the man I had known and respected so much. I cursed myself for passing on gossip and being self-serving while doing it. I heard myself suggest that I knew more about Philip's life than I did, and that I was a more intimate friend than I had been. My desire to impress Storr appalled me, and I knew I had made a fool of myself.

When the subject of Philip and Musa's marriage came up, I melodramatically asked that the tape recorder be turned off. Storr did this, expecting, no doubt, some equally melodramatic revelation. Just after Musa's stroke, Philip told me that while there had been one or two students he had slept with at Iowa after that he never . . . Storr stopped me. He had already spoken with several women who claimed to have slept with Philip. Even this exposure of my vanity didn't slow me down, and after Storr turned the tape recorder back on, I continued to suggest my friendship with Philip had been deeper than in fact it had been. In my guilt the next morning, the memory of my running off at the mouth killed whatever intimations I may have had about doing a book on Guston.

But as the years passed I began to think that I had things to say about Guston and his work, the late work in particular, that either were not being said or needed to be said again with the emphasis I could give them. Besides, I had thought so hard about Guston's work and talked at such length about it that I wanted to put everything into words on paper and thus find out what I really thought. When I began this book, and through the first few drafts, I was naive and did not realize that Guston was in the room with me and that I was trying to please him as I wrote.

As I worked, it struck me that I had placed myself in a position Guston knew well. I quote in this book the conversation he once had with John Cage during which Cage described how Guston's studio was filled with the past, his friends, and the art world, when he entered and began to paint. Guston learned, as Cage said, that he had to show everyone the door, and when *he* (Guston) left, painting could really begin. I came to know what Cage meant, and began to understand something of the ruthlessness you must employ to create. To get the Guston and his work I know on paper, for knowing him did not end with his death, I had to end my conversation with him. I could not worry about offending him or presenting him in an unfavorable light, nor could I argue his case for him. In the end, I think I got him far enough out the door so that I was free to write the book I did not know I was going to write when I began. To be in a state of such uncertainty and to somehow find your way is appropriate, I came to see, for someone writing about Philip Guston.

Part One

I love all men who dive. Any fish can swim near the surface, but it takes a great whale to go downstairs five miles or more; & if he doesn't attain the bottom, why all the lead in Galena can't fashion the plummet that will.

— HERMAN MELVILLE TO EVERT DUYCKINCK

Marlborough Gallery, October 1970

At the opening two painters, David Hare and Bill de Kooning, acted differently. It wasn't necessarily that they liked it. De Kooning said something else. He said, "Why are they all complaining about your making political art, all this talk? You know what your real subject is, it's about freedom, to be free, the artist's first duty."

At the opening he (de Kooning) grabbed me, hugged me, and said he was envious, which was flattering because I regarded him as the best painter in the country and, in many ways, the only one, I mean he's a real mind and a real painter. "Philip," he said, "this isn't the subject. Do you know what the real subject is?" And we both said at the same time, "Freedom." Then we hugged each other again. Of course that's what it's about. Freedom. That's the only possession the artist has — Freedom to do whatever he can imagine.

The other important thing de Kooning said to me was, "Well, now you are on your own. You've paid off all your debts! Now you are on your own."

As Philip Guston's friend over the last eight years of his life, I heard these versions and others of what Willem de Kooning said that afternoon at the Marlborough Gallery. For Guston, de Kooning's cry of freedom became a talisman. He invoked it as a way of dispelling the mean-spirited attacks that met this first show of his late work and of justifying his new course as it took its several surprising turns. De Kooning's remark meant to Guston that he was embarked in the right direction even as he had no clear sense where that might lead. To Guston, freedom signified both freedom from his past and freedom for the present and future. Between his 1966 show at New York's Jewish Museum and the Marlborough opening, Guston reinvented himself as a painter. He did so in isolation, showing hardly any new paintings in New York. He leapt, or so it appeared, from the coal black, blocky, headlike masses on wintry gray grounds to blood-spattered Ku Klux Klansmen riding around in roadsters, raising hell and proud of it. He went from a dirge to a Bronx cheer. This book will explore the routes he took during those four years, but viewers who first saw these hooded figures at Marlborough had no road map. Guston's late work burst on them, sending a shock through the gallery, disturbing admirers and critics alike.

There were no bridge paintings in the show, no images that showed Guston struggling to leave one world for this radical other. The painter his public thought it knew was not the painter whose work now hung at Marlborough. It was as if he went to sleep as one sort of painter and awoke as another. Guston's past was, as would become more obvious with each show, emphatically over.

Critics and friends questioned Guston's motives and his judgment. Had he sold out to Pop Art? Were these cartoon images a crass bid for notoriety? A detour? A stunning lapse? Was Guston slumming? Did these images mean that he had abandoned abstract painting or that it had abandoned him? De Kooning brushed aside all speculation. In emphasizing the artist's duty to himself, he affirmed Guston's intuition that this work was inevitable. Guston well knew that concepts of choice and will could not begin to explain where the hoods and pink cities came from. Those who attempted to handicap this work as an entry in an imagined abstract/pop horse race simply confirmed his disdain for the art world. If that world saw things in terms of strategies and career moves what could it tell him about what he had done?

6

Guston had slammed the door on his past, and in 1970 his future looked bleak, at least by the standards of the art world he was kissing off. Few of the new paintings sold, and the reviews were by and large memorable for their low blows laid on as much in rancorous disappointment as in anger. Hilton Kramer's venomous "From Mandarin to Stumblebum" in *The New York Times* earned him a place in Guston's history. By 1972 Guston was without a gallery. He quit Marlborough, trucking his paintings to his Woodstock, New York, home and studio. Although he was stung by the resistance to his new work, Guston's leave-taking was not sour grapes alone. He turned away from the New York art scene he had already left in spirit.

Guston never hid the hurt he felt over the incomprehension of friends, the critical hatchet jobs, and the common wisdom that he had betrayed his gifts, his life as a painter. Since it never occurred to him to turn back, to meet others' expectations, and because of his natural inclination to brood, Guston dwelt on this hurt and found use for it. It refined and shaped his thoughts about the world and the painting he had left behind. A package of negative reviews reached him, the "Xerox underground" he called it, in Venice, and after reading them and feeling glad he was not the painter his critics wanted him to be, he dumped the package in a canal. He liked to remember this moment as he liked to quote de Kooning, but the frequency of the telling suggests how much the initial reception of his late work rankled him.

One moral of the Venice story is that the embattled artist can become stronger, and Guston gloried in battle. But to be embattled in this way the artist must be recognized; the neglected artist has neither the adversaries nor the advantages for dealing with them fame brings. Guston, I think, needed fame so as to reject it. It is unsurprising that he used vitriolic reviews as a spur, but he had a similar contempt and use for much of the attention that came his way. This was a man who later on, as he hid out in his Woodstock, New York, home for long periods of time, had a switch installed on his telephone so he could turn it off. He was proud of this switch, proud that he could evade the world that pursued him, and proud, I think, to be pursued. He hated those reviews but he took strength from them. Silence might have left him alone in Venice with too many of his own thoughts.

Doubt was always central to Guston's process, and now he was free to work from his doubts. Free to discover what he knew to be inside him but had never before imagined and to "baffle," his word, himself in doing so. He had, the reception of the Marlborough show proved to him, no one but himself to please. Now he finished many a night's work spooked by what he had painted, needing to sleep it off. In the mornings he returned to see what he had left in his studio, and he could be rattled by what he saw, shocked enough to hustle his wife, Musa, into the studio so she could marvel at what he had painted.

In the decade beginning in 1970 Guston went on numerous runs of painting, producing an enormous body of work for a painter of any age but for a man in his sixties, astonishing! He had the energy of Picasso. Guston was, with the constraint that true freedom insists on, open to be seized by images that he came to think of as "breeding," as he described the process, having a life of their own. They freely metamorphosed, and Guston had no more explanation for this than Gregor Samsa did for why he woke one morning as a bug. One moment Guston saw himself as a movie director in charge of his images and the next as a victim, a willing victim, of an onslaught of images. His hand was free to connect with his mind, a circuit beyond interference. What he imagined, he painted and what he painted as often as not astounded him.

Guston's fifties soul mate, the composer Morton Feldman, was one of those who for whatever reason could not "see" Guston's late work. Their friendship foundered. In the midseventies Guston painted a portrait of Feldman, *Friend — to M.F.* Feldman, who had turned away from Guston, is turned three quarters away from the viewer. The ear that shows is large as the Buddha's. Feldman smokes. His is a monumental, fleshy head rising from naked shoulders so physically there that Guston has summoned his friend back in paint.

8

In the end Feldman did embrace Guston's late work, and he wrote a catalog essay for the very last paintings that closes on a note echoing de Kooning's cry of freedom, a note made poignant by Guston and Feldman's long estrangement. "There is," Feldman wrote, "no attempt at reconciliation with his past concerns. It was a new life, in which his past skills helped him on the new ground he emigrated to. All it meant for Guston was to pack only what he needed to go in search of his heart."

One of Guston's last images is a battered, much soldered and patched teakettle. It could have been Mother Courage's kettle or the one carried from Odessa to Montreal by Guston's immigrant family. The kettle's spout resembles a bird's beak, joyously chirping the steam that pours up from it. It is whistling, cheerful, defiant — I have come through!

When this drawing came in a letter from Guston, I had never seen the character and could not identify the original artist. Over the years those I asked drew a blank. By chance the artist and musician Stephen Fredette saw the drawing and knew Slim Jim's creator to be Frink, just Frink. He drew the cartoon in the first decades of this century and is now a footnote in books on American comic art.

Part Two

The act of painting is like a trial where all the roles are lived by one person. It's as if the painting has to prove its right to exist. There are enough paintings in the world. Life and art have a mutual contempt and necessity for each other.

— PHILIP GUSTON

hilip Guston was born Philip Goldstein, youngest of seven children, in Montreal, Canada, in 1913. His parents, Lewis and Rachel, were refugees from Odessa's brutal pogroms that followed the suppression of the sailors' mutiny aboard the *Potemkin*. In his last decade Guston fancied Odessa as his true birthplace and source of his imagination. Thanking me for a book by Isaac Babel, chronicler of Odessa's Jewish life and underworld, Guston wrote two months before his death in 1980, "His (Babel's) work is magic — a miracle. What he leaves out — what he puts in — creates a real touchable world — he is truly miraculous. I hope to be like him. Could it be that Odessa is not a fantasy at all — in my blood somehow?"

The Goldstein family stayed six years in Montreal, where Lewis worked as a machinist for the Canadian railroad. If these six years left, as they must have, significant impressions on Guston, no one has yet written about them, and he never spoke of Montreal to me. In 1919 the family moved to Los Angeles, and the next year, according to Robert Storr, or in 1923 or 1924 according to Guston's daughter, Musa (this discrepancy will have to be resolved by Guston's biographer), Lewis Goldstein hanged himself from a shed rafter. It was Guston who discovered his father.

What little we know of Guston's early life and adolescence comes to us shaped by his later achievements as a painter and is now surrounded with the glow of legend. He began drawing at twelve, and his mother, recognizing his talent, gave him a correspondence course to the Cleveland School of Cartooning. He didn't keep up with this but continued to draw on his own, often, as he liked to recount, squirreling himself away in a closet to draw under a naked lightbulb.

13

In high school he made friends with classmate Jackson Pollock and encountered an extraordinary teacher, Frederick John de St. Vrain Schwankovsky, who introduced them to cubism and Oriental philosophy. In 1928 Guston and Pollock were expelled from school for their role in a broadside satirizing the English department. Guston never returned, and except for three months at Los Angeles's Otis Art Institute, his formal education ended at fifteen. This seems the history of a born painter.

Not that Guston painted pictures before he turned fifteen. Painting is an art without prodigies, and he was no exception. But Guston had begun to train himself through imitation. He traced the cartoons of Piero della Francesca frescoes and those of other Renaissance masters at the Los Angeles Public Library. In 1930, when he was seventeen, Guston saw Walter and Louise Arensberg's collection of modern paintings and his first painting by de Chirico, an artist he loved throughout his life. Few Americans living outside New York had the opportunity to see such modern European paintings. Guston's gifts had the good fortune of an encouraging mother, the luck of high school friendships and of living in a city where a great deal was going on.

Hollywood was, for one, the only place where he could work as an extra in the movies. In 1931 he played an artist at work in his studio, and in another movie he played a high priest. Perhaps Guston would have become a passionate moviegoer had he not grown up near Hollywood, but his early exposure to movies seems as crucial to his development as a painter as his more written about mural painting in Mexico. Copying Piero's *The Story of the True Cross*, Guston could imagine Piero as a movie director, especially in the battle scenes, a detail of which hung in his Woodstock studio fifty years later. The shift up in scale of American abstract painters is commonly seen as coming naturally from their work on WPA murals. But what of the movie screen? Its dimension and the power of the images cast upon it must have had an impact on the first generation of painters to go to the movies.

Guston's lifelong appetite for American popular culture did not begin with "Krazy Kat," alone, the cartoon so often associated with his late work, now somewhat highbrow itself, but with the movies and the vivid, zany Los Angeles culture that, for instance, so turned on Nathanael West. Guston told me of going to see Aimee Semple McPherson preach in her International Church of the Foursquare Gospel, the lighted cross of which he could see from his bedroom. He sat in the back pew with the old gaffers and no accounts who were there, as he was, to catch a glimpse of Aimee's wiggle in her clinging white satin dress. McPherson roared up the aisle on her motorcycle, stopping when the traffic light on the altar turned red. She leapt from her cycle, flung aloft her open hand. "Stop sinners!" she cried, "in the name of the Lord!"

You can get the feel of American vulgarity anywhere in the country, but even then Los Angeles, especially then as the movie industry began to heat up, had a leg up. When I say the word *movie*, I can feel this vulgarity in my mouth.

The earliest surviving Guston painting is *Mother and Child*, dated 1930. He claimed to have used house paint, and in reproduction the painting shows a yellowish cast as house paint will, but I recently saw it close-up, and the colors are bright and the paint silky. Clearly, the heroic mother and her child descend from Picasso's classical figures. Guston painted them with conviction, and they are powerfully expressive, but looked at from the whole of his career the subject is of little interest. It is the background details that hold this viewer's attention. Here is a brick wall, a chair, its wood grain lovingly detailed, and floorboards, all images that recur forty years later. As Guston told Dore Ashton in 1974, he came to see his work as "circular" in that "like Babel I want to paint things long forgotten." The hooded figures, lengths of hangman's rope, and brick walls of the lost painting *Conspirators* of 1931 are among those forgotten things to be remembered in the late sixties. If "Krazy Kat's" horizon lines and flung bricks haunt Guston's late work, so do the productions of his youth.

15

But in 1931 *Conspirators* had another meaning. It hung in Guston's first one-man show at Stanley Rose's Los Angeles Bookshop. At about the same time, Guston joined a John Reed Club, where Marxist politics dominated. Responding to the injustice done the Scottsboro Boys, Guston and others painted a group of portable frescoes to be shown outdoors at rallies. A Guston panel showed two black youths about to be lynched, which is exactly what the hooded figures in his *Conspirators* are up to. When a police "Red Squad" raided the John Reed Club, all the frescoes were defaced, shot up, Guston said, slashed and destroyed. In one of Guston's panels the cops shot holes in the black figure's eyes and genitals.

Thus Guston experienced early and at firsthand sanctioned political violence. The "Red Squad" attack on his paintings was so significant to his political education that an account of it appears in every book written on him. In the streets of Los Angeles his education continued as he watched the revived Ku Klux Klan parade, a sight that as a Jew must have chilled and frightened him. Following the war and civil rights news in the late sixties, his instincts told him there was a conspiracy, and he remembered the marching Klansmen. Enjoying each new Watergate revelation and talking over every reported detail of that conspiracy's ins and outs in my kitchen, he described Nixon and his minions as Klansmen in a new guise.

Back in Los Angeles he worked for a furrier, drove a truck, labored in a factory, and is remembered for having dressed well. We know he could afford to as he was making good money working for his brothers. There was, I bring this up to emphasize, little of the bohemian about Guston as a youth or in old age. Nearly fifty years later, on the last night I saw him alive, he wore new clothes from, he proudly pointed out, Brooks Brothers: green twill trousers, a blackwatch plaid shirt, and over it one of the sweater-shirts, collar up, he favored. Guston had not dressed this well on previous Boston visits, but he had a sense of style, a bit of theater, that showed in small gestures like the upturned shirt collar and the flourishes by which he emphasized his ever-present cigarettes.

That Guston worked hard at many jobs as a youth comes as no surprise. He came from a large family of hardworking immigrants. In contrast to his fellow painters, he lived a fairly settled life. His friend Pollock became a notorious and pathetic roaring boy; Franz Kline had nearly as many addresses as the 714 the Japanese painter Hokusai is said to have had; de Kooning had a daughter out of wedlock, but Guston had a family, teaching jobs, and, from the early forties, a base at Woodstock. He sweated away at his art like a bourgeois, just as flaubert had done. Indeed, at various times in his life and especially in his last decade, he lived to work and arranged things so as to eliminate all interference. He did not, in contrast to the equally workaholic de Kooning, have an assistant. Another person in the studio could have been only a distraction.

In 1932 Guston encountered the Mexican muralists David Alfaro Siquieros and José Clemente Orozco, then at work in Los Angeles. In 1934, in company with two friends, he traveled to Morelia, Mexico, where, with Siquieros as their sponsor, they painted a mural in the former emperor Maxmilian's palace. Upon completing this, Guston returned to Los Angeles and worked on another mural before joining the WPA's Federal Arts Project. That winter Guston left Los Angeles for New York, seldom to return and rarely to see his family again. Pollock had preceded him, and for a time Guston camped out in his apartment. They were probably closer during these weeks than they would ever be again. Guston soon found work with the WPA and met Gorky, de Kooning, Stuart Davis, James Brooks, and a host of other artists at work in the city. He visited museums and galleries, reaffirming his love for de Chirico at a Pierre Matisse Gallery show. In 1937, now a New Yorker, he married Musa McKim, an artist and poet, whom he had first met during his brief time at the Otis Art Institute. Guston was twenty-four.

Few Gustons exist from the thirties. He painted murals in Georgia, in Queens, New York, and, with his wife, the still visible murals in Laconia, New Hampshire, and Binghamton, New York. We have drawings, but he had little time for easel painting. In New York this was a decade of talk, and Guston concentrated on educating himself in conversations with fellow painters, at museums and galleries, and on one memorable occasion spying on Stuart Davis. Guston had a studio next to Davis, and hearing the older painter at work he hoisted himself over a makeshift wall and peered at him. Davis did little more than scrape off a mass of paint, but this "waste" of paint impressed Guston, and he used the anecdote to illustrate his conviction that you must be free to abandon what you are doing. The artist's first allegiance is to his vision. If a painting goes wrong it's not his duty to make it come out right but to recognize the error and begin again no matter how much paint is scraped to the floor. Since paint was expensive in the thirties, the extravagance of Davis's act impressed this lesson on Guston.

In a generation of American painters who had little formal training, Guston stands out as a self-made artist. De Kooning had the advantage of his Dutch school education. Kline had studied in England, and Pollock apprenticed himself to Thomas Hart Benton, but Guston had only his short tenure at despised Otis. Before he left there he piled all the plaster casts he was supposed to be drawing in a heap and drew the jumble this made. There are late drawings of hillsides strewn with junk that circle back to this, a link he several times emphasized, image of his anger at what he considered the meaningless demands placed upon him.

Guston's generation of American painters, to a man immigrants to New York, discovered there the vision and drive to lift American painting to a world-class art in the fifties. Not that they did more than imagine this in the thirties. Few of the painters had shows, and only a handful of paintings sold. But the WPA paid well enough to keep most of the painters in New York, where they could live cheaply and draw on one another's company. They had no art market to keep up with or satisfy. In retrospect that world seems more innocent than it could have been, but the painters did have the advantage of educating themselves in the culture of painting and not in the marketplace.

Guston's self-education needs emphasizing because it set his course. From the start he struggled not with teachers and academic demands — he simply ignored these — but with himself. This meant he got no nourishment from the approval of teachers. When he studied reproductions of the Italian Renaissance masters, he did so out of his instinct that it was right for him. He always gave me the feeling that he had mastered his art on his own, but he did enjoy fortunate circumstances. His mural work gave him, as it did his colleagues, a public forum and the wherewithal to sustain himself without the pressure of a public career. He had what now seems the luxury of coming of age slowly, of debating and thinking through perplexing questions — the problem of flatness in painting, for instance — alone and with others of like passion and dedication. Even so, for all the camaraderie of the period, Guston went his own way. By nature he was a brooder who could not help but look at every side of any question. Then, while others tore their hair out, he would look again. He never lost this sometimes maddening habit of intellectual interrogation. In conversation you would just think you had gotten somewhere when Guston, with a single question, would wipe out the distance you had come and you were back at square one. Ideas never struck him like lightning. He had to, as he repeatedly insisted, "live" his paintings.

In 1940 he began to concentrate on easel painting. He fulfilled mural commissions until 1942, but by then, 1941 to be exact, he had completed the picture he considered his first mature work, *Martial Memory*. Guston finished this painting in Iowa City, Iowa, where he taught through the war years until 1945.

I have no idea how Guston came to teach at Iowa. I never asked, and he never said. Dore Ashton has Guston "offered" the post, so Iowa must have courted him. It is easy to imagine him being interested in getting out of New York. As much as he got from the city, he thrived away from it and enjoyed not having to be dependent upon it. In any case he was one of the first of his contemporaries to take up teaching full-time and make a parallel career of it, something de Kooning, Kline, Pollock, and Mark Rothko never did. As much as Guston cursed his lot and itched to flee teaching, he built an excellent reputation as a teacher, one that sustained him during his last decade.

And so Guston went to the Midwest, where he remained, St. Louis after Iowa, until 1947. While abstract painting heated up in New York, Guston was out of it, in the hinterlands working on what were to some of his New York friends conventional pictures. Pollock, for one, damned them and damned Guston for betraying the cause of abstract painting. Guston was going against the grain, and with great labor, as he painted very slowly during these years, he produced paintings that made a name for themselves. These were scenes in which children are prominent: they play war in *Martial Memory*, are costumed for a party or carnival in *If This Be Not I*, and in *Sanctuary* a sleepless boy agonizes in bed, the city outside his window. In 1944 Guston had his first solo show. In 1945 he had his first one-man show in New York. De Kooning, who was painting abstractly and suffered accordingly, did not have his first one-man show until 1948.

Prizes came Guston's way: firsts in painting at a Carnegie Institute show and at a show in Richmond, Virginia. The May 1946 *Life* ran a substantial article on him, three years before the magazine turned its attention to Jackson Pollock — "Pollock: Is He the Greatest Living American Painter?" This article left Pollock feeling "like a rabbit in the headlights of an oncoming car," a glare from which he could not escape. Guston, on the other hand, got his measure of early fame for work he would soon repudiate.

In 1947 Guston won a Guggenheim, allowing him to take leave from Washington University in St. Louis and move to Woodstock, New York, where he completed *Porch No. 2*, his last figurative work until the late sixties. It is a painting in which boards, a rope, legs, and the soles and heels of shoes are prominent.

Guston's moody, poetic paintings of children, a synthesis of Max Beckmann, Uccello (the groupings of the figures), and de Chirico (the melancholy cityscapes in which the action takes place), clearly found favor with prize juries and fellowship boards. Guston was, by their standards, a successful painter, far more successful than his contemporaries painting abstract paintings in New York. The art world, which sustained so few of his New York colleagues, sustained him. In 1948 he won both a Prix de Rome and $1,000 from the American Academy of Arts and Letters. This largesse allowed him to go to Rome and travel through Italy, France, and Spain for the first time. This grant support also coincided with Guston's three-year inching into abstraction — three paintings finished between 1947 and 1950. When he returned to figuration twenty years later, he followed a similar pattern — much time spent away from New York City and a visit to Italy.

In turning away from figuration, Guston turned his back on a style that had brought him considerable success. While his New York colleagues broke down barriers and brought abstraction into the mainstream, Guston was a latecomer who, oddly enough, arrived at abstraction through Europe. In Rome as he worked on the abstract *Tormentors* (a loaded title for this transitional painting), he saw the masterpieces of his youth in the flesh for the first time and took inspiration from them. The art he saw influenced him, he later told me, to follow his own impulses. On his way home, in a Paris hotel room, he did a series of small gouaches in which he further worked out his new vocabulary.

Since his wife remained at home for most of this year, Guston was alone. Turning away from success in solitude became his way. In the late sixties he again bit the hand that had fed him liberally and did so in isolation in the Catskills, making work that rejected and condemned the art world and, not incidentally, the work of his recent past. Guston's conversions had to be total. Embracing a new way of painting meant forswearing the old.

There is in this record the paradox of wanting to please, wanting acclaim, while simultaneously, and with equal energy, seeking a private vision no public approval could sustain. fielding Dawson remembers a Guston watercolor illustrating an early fifties Container Corporation of America advertisement, and the hope that this gave him and his fellow Black Mountain students that their art might find a place in the world. Guston had this hope, but he came to want that place only on his own terms. The painter Jean Hélion said of Balthus, "He wanted to get out of modern art. He wanted to get out, and he wanted to get in. And he succeeded." The same can be said of Guston.

(Lest I give the impression that Guston's forties and fifties were all that grand . . . despite the prizes and grants and regular New York shows, increasing critical and public attention for both his paintings and abstract painting in general, Guston, according to Robert Storr's account, sold eleven paintings, fewer than one a year, from 1941 to 1956.)

During these years Guston typified for some, Clement Greenberg was one, the romantic artist at war with his time. "Darkly handsome," the common phrase, into middle age, he certainly looked the part. He was deep in the art world yet shunned it and broadcast his contradictory thoughts and feelings. He was embattled, a "fighter against his time" (Dore Ashton must have pleased Guston when she chose these words from Nietzsche as a motto for her book, *Yes, but . . .*) who knew his time intimately and waged his battles in public through his art, the late work most particularly. With his gift for self-dramatization, Guston elevated his personal struggles to make art into mighty battles. His wife, Musa, once acerbically observed that anyone who listened to Guston could be his friend. Certainly, I know from our many late night conversations how much he needed a sympathetic ear and how hard he listened to himself. At times I felt along for the ride, excited by his talk and aware that he talked, in part, to hear himself think out loud.

It was not in Guston's character to let up, to take it easy on the world or himself. Exasperating to some, heroic to others, certainly heroic to me, as brilliant as he was mordant and touchy, Guston had the curse of never being able to leave well enough alone. This might have frozen him, and perhaps it explains the slow transition from abstraction to figuration, but over the years he turned it to his advantage. By the time I met him doubt was integral to his process, and that was one of the great lessons I learned from him. I had thought doubt signified a killing weakness. If you doubted what you were doing how could you do it? Guston's ability to be in doubt but not compromised or destroyed by it and to value uncertainty for the inspiring, if anxiety producing, tension it created is what Keats meant by "Negative Capability, that is when man is capable of being in uncertainties, Mysteries, doubts without any irritable reaching after fact & reason."

Those who knew Guston in New York during the fifties remember his wild mood swings. One night he might show up at the Cedar Bar in despair, sure he was not a painter, so down he carried everyone with him. A few nights later he would breeze in all smiles, joyous, ready to be the life of the party, and such was his charm that everyone's spirits lifted. He had just brought off a painting and all was right with the world. I do not think I saw him that down or that up, but in either mood he gave a charge that fit an evening of food, drink, and talk.

The painter Al Held once told me Guston drove him crazy during the fifties because he was "such a kvetch," he could not let the mildest casual statement about painting pass without worrying it to death. Guston had a constant complaint, it seemed to Held, that he could resolve only by annihilating it in talk. To his close friend Morton Feldman Guston was "the arch crank. Very little satisfied him. Very little art. Always aware in his own work of the rhetorical nature of the complication. Guston reduces, reduces building his own tower of Babel and then destroys it."

Feldman's "the rhetorical nature of the complication" is an apt phrase. Guston's demons were in perpetual discourse, and this discourse was itself a demon. Of course these demons did not appear only in Guston's studio. He brought them home with him, and he was fascinated by his own difficult behavior and the cunning rationalizations he developed to fuel steamrolling arguments that proved him the injured party. He was also fascinated by how other artists dealt with their often volatile natures. He proudly told me that he had it from Pierre Matisse that the great Matisse himself swept the dinner dishes to the floor after a frustrating day at the studio even though the family was staying in a hotel and all could hear the crash of broken crockery. And Guston loved to hear my own accounts of similar explosions. No art, it seems, could arise without complication.

Odd then that beginning with *White Painting* (1950), his first totally abstract picture, and continuing through the fifties, Guston's best work is serene at its core. I am thinking of *Attar, Beggar's Joys,* and the Museum of Modern Art's *Painting*. Guston came, I believe, to distrust this serenity and the beauty of these pictures, but for a time serenity and beauty ruled.

Guston achieved this by limiting his palette, concentrating on cadmium red medium (his color), composing his webs of short brush strokes just off center, and surrounding these bright, cloudlike figures with a sort of weather or memory of paintings unresolved, the trails from which the action emerges. The brush strokes, at times crosshatched, are quietly agitated — the drawings of this period, early to midfifties, are fiercely so — but agitated like rain.

These pictures invite contemplation. Something (a recognizable image?) is forming or is in the process of dissolution. This in-betweenness gathers the viewer in delicately but with all the command of a Mondrian. You're knocked over by a feather. Whatever the tumult in Guston's thinking about painting, these paintings are resolved. They contain their own history in the space around the edges that tells us they have come from somewhere. They have the dignity of refusing to choose between alternatives, of allowing contrary impulses to coexist. Their mind may not be entirely made up, but it is a sensuous mind, appealing and open to the viewer's eye.

In 1949 Guston did a few realistic drawings of street scenes on the island of Ischia. One of these, sometimes identified as *Drawing No. 2 (Ischia),* is a signature image. It is reproduced in numerous books on Guston and was among the drawings he chose for the 1977 drawing retrospective at the David McKee Gallery. There is a stone wall to the left leading up to the packed arrangement of stone buildings, houses on top of one another, typical of Italian hill towns. Their placement on the paper, a little to the right and "in," as if you are walking up the main village street, summons the viewer in the same way Guston's fifties abstractions do. *Attar* does not represent a village street, but the same invitation is there.

In 1957 and 1958 Guston went in a new direction. Black appears as a dominant color. His brush strokes are longer and wider. Patches of blue, orange, and green hold forth, and the paint is thicker, plastered on. A certain exquisiteness of touch has disappeared. The air that surrounded earlier clusters of paint has been used up, and these pictures rise to the surface with propulsive force. They are named *Dial* and *The Clock*, and one from 1958 is *To Fellini*, whose movies Guston adored. The shapes at the center of these paintings form a sort of emblem. Looked at from the vantage point of his late work, these paintings seem to contain unformed or suppressed realistic images. *Painter* must, with hindsight, present a painter at his easel. So radically does Guston's work change over time that it is hard not to search for constants, to impose an order and progression and make the totality of his career come out nice and even.

Whatever the content of these paintings, there is a new boldness in the way Guston handles paint. His brush strokes are expansive; the forms they create are larger, bulkier, and less balanced. These pictures are no longer composed slightly off center. They are all over, smeared and pushed with the paint aggressively up front. There is no seductive in-between.

In 1958 the Ford Foundation gave Guston $10,000. This freed him from teaching, to which he did not return regularly until 1973. In these fourteen years he had a retrospective, before Pollock, Kline, de Kooning, and Rothko, at the Guggenheim; showed radically new dark paintings at the Jewish Museum in 1966; then removed himself from New York for the four years it took to remake himself as a painter.

These overlooked midsixties paintings shown at the Jewish Museum deserve a word or two. They were hammered by the critics, and Guston seemed to give up on them as he had scant space for them in his 1980 retrospective. Of course he wanted the room for his late paintings, but Harry Hopkins, who organized the show, pushed for what Guston called his "dark pictures." Guston recalled playing a "card game" in which Hopkins raised him a "dark picture."

Two late paintings, Guston called him. Two dark paintings? Four late works! . . . Guston got his way, and only five "dark pictures" were in the ninety-eight works, fifty-three of which were from Guston's last twelve years.

Painted over five years and in all seasons, these dark pictures are set in perpetual winter. The gray grounds are luminous and stormy. Behind and to the edges of these, pink might show through, like a rising or declining winter sun. Or the blue of a winter sky or plummy depths like autumn bayberry or ocher blazing like metal. Guston smeared his gray around, and its storminess comes from the abandon, like a rolling boil, with which the paint is slathered on.

Set more on top of this storm than in it are rough black, night black, pitch black, shapes. Some are hunks or nuggets of coal, but many are squarish head shapes, either alone (several are titled *Portrait*) or two forming a company. Looking at a painting in which two such shapes are close together, Guston pointed out, "This one is telling the other his troubles."

And troubled is what these heads, stuck in their gelid gray weather, are. But there is no hint at the source of this trouble. The dread these pictures broadcast may come from the isolation of the heads, from their black depression. It may, but this dread seems of the pure twentieth-century strain, dread more powerful because you cannot put your finger on its cause. Not that Guston needed to know. He could manufacture enough dread on his own. Perhaps he inherited a vulnerability to such torment from his suicide-father. In any case, Guston had a direct line to that shadow of doom, that storm that never breaks, that state we took Kafka's name to describe, and in whose thrall our nervous system does double time.

And yet, as so often with Guston's art, the paint suggests another, contradictory, reading of these pictures. It has been laid on with such assurance, so lavishly, and beams forth a pearl's luster, the palpable luster of fog, that it is hard to agree with Bill Berkson that "duress is their theme." But Berkson has caught the heaviness that glides in on the paint. It is never a matter of either/or with Guston but either and or. The skin of paint, joy of its going on, is one with the pervasive disquiet the form compels us to feel. The fulcrum in these pictures may be the mind's refusal to completely accept what the hand can do.

In their murk and gloom, the troubled and troubling confusion of their forms, these dark pictures recall the handful of paintings Guston completed in the late forties, as he moved at a snail's pace into abstraction. *Red Painting* (1950) is so dark it looks like it needs a cleaning after years hanging in a smoky tavern. The black shapes, brothers to those in the dark pictures, are nearly drowned in a red the color of dried blood. It is a painting at odds with itself, refusing to declare its intentions. We know the declaration will be for abstraction, but *Red Painting* has not arrived at this. The dark pictures of the midsixties are also burying one world. Their blacks are the void into which the impulse to more abstractions will be sucked. No wonder Guston stopped painting for a few years after finishing this series.

Even in the Guston abstractions I find serene there is what he identified in the work of his friend Bradley Walker Tomlin, "an anguished sense of alternatives." Perhaps the anguish and the multitude of alternatives, the need to maintain the tension in his abstractions, got to Guston. Perhaps, and this is said from the perilous ledge of hindsight inevitable in writing about Guston's career, abstraction never fulfilled him. He did feel that his late work took his full measure, heard promptings ignored. Looking back from the late work, Guston's abstract years seem both preparatory and a sidetrack, a turn into a dreamt of and hoped for purity that his demands on painting and the demand painting made on him could not uphold. There is no lack of commitment or care in these abstract paintings. Indeed, Guston gave himself so completely to these impulses that he used them up, and discovered they had not touched his core. Brave of him to accept this truth, to stop doing what he could do so well, and how hard such acceptance must have been.

In the hierarchy of abstract painters Guston is often ranked below de Kooning, Kline, and Pollock and even below Rothko. Guston's late work seems to distract some critics. They argue that he returned to figuration because he could not paint first-rate abstractions. He left, the implication is, the company of heroes because he could not measure up. Others enlarge this to claim that Guston climbed on the bandwagon of abstraction, that he came late and his heart was never in it. They cite his condemnation of abstraction as evidence.

Neither argument is sound. Guston questioned the premise of abstract painting even while deeply involved in such painting, because he was so involved. "There is something ridiculous," he said in 1960, "and miserly in the myth we inherit from abstract art that painting is autonomous, pure and for itself. Therefore we habitually analyze its ingredients and define its limits." Guston's paintings embody this interrogation and a parallel frustration with the limiting terms of the abstract case at hand. If they do not wrestle with us, throw their net over us, and pin us through force of will as Pollock's do; if they do not soar as the great de Koonings of the late fifties and early sixties do; and if they lack Kline's daring and simplicity, this means Guston's strengths and virtues are elsewhere.

Guston's abstractions are in-drawing. Their refined touch, as often disparaged as celebrated, is like a beguiling voice, one that you must draw close to if you want to catch every word and nuance. Through scale, stroke, and delicacy of color, tones of rose and gray, these paintings create intimacy, an intimacy you will not find in the gorgeous billboards of de Kooning, Pollock, and Kline. Yet these Gustons do not give themselves up easily, and the viewer must proceed into their interior on his own. This is especially true of the early fifties paintings. These concentrate an essence, an irreducible experience, and many could be rightly called, as a noble one is, *Attar.*

As Guston's abstractions evolved, his forms grew bolder, the paint and light crowd to the surface. These paintings of the late fifties and early sixties are, in Guston's phrase, "image ridden." The weather that once surrounded the core of his pictures has blown in bolder shapes to seize the center and spread to the edges. The emotions are more acted out than implied, and there is a rougher embrace. Then came the dark pictures, with their cellarlike, dusk light inhabited by simple, eloquent forms.

What I see in Guston's abstractions is an imagination constantly attempting new combinations while questioning the entire enterprise. For me the great charge of abstract painting is in its faith that when the imagination engages paint's pure matter and light anything can happen. It is a fountain that overflows, an art without restraint, except, as so came to trouble Guston, that the image is exiled. Guston's abstractions contain the promise that animated a generation of American artists. Looked at over time they always lift me to a new plane, a world where light, color, and form cohere to aerate mind and heart. Guston's painted world refreshes and intensifies the world I live in. That the same can be said of Piero, Corot, or Courbet is as it should be.

Only hard looking will support my conviction that Guston's abstract paintings are of the first rank, but the bandwagon tag has nothing to do with looking. What difference does it make when a painting was painted? We have been sold the myth of heroic abstract painting, and from this arises the idea of a bandwagon. The first to commit themselves totally to abstraction were the first to suffer and thus the first to be ennobled. After de Kooning, Pollock, and Kline the way was smooth: there was now a style and masters of that style. And so abstraction is a movement or campaign, a political campaign, with a beginning, middle, and end and prize ribbons to be handed out by art historians/critics who will keep things in order. Abstract art, all this implies, could not survive its beginnings. The race was over while it was being run.

Guston's insistent, stinging criticism of this myth was, characteristically, self-criticism. If he was right that abstraction's "only subject is itself," then his work of more than fifteen years must be judged by the thinness he decried in all abstraction. How silly the bandwagon seems next to this level of analysis.

At age fifty-three in 1966, with the Jewish Museum show behind him, Guston had no idea what was next. He was no stranger to uncertainty; indeed, the condition appealed to him. He claimed he aspired to be "baffled." At this point he had a career to depend on and a reputation to protect him, but how quickly what you know, what you can do can look flimsy, obvious, and done to death. You have just moved an inch or lived another day, yet from where you now stand your art is moribund, hopeless of renewal. This does not happen to every artist, but it happened to Guston. He could have willed these intuitions away, returned to what he knew and gone on with his work. But Guston had to begin again.

In 1967 he moved permanently to Woodstock, New York, his summer home and escape hatch since 1947. He thought he was leaving behind, and gleefully so, the art world that had, on balance, been good to him. He was a successful painter, not that success mattered to him. Well, it did matter. He always knew where he stood and was not without personal ambition, but he also believed that success never taught him as much as frustration and failure. His art was, over the next three years, to demand and exact more from him than ever before, more stamina, greater daring, patience, and reserves of faith to counter persistent doubt. He was about to begin again. Eleven years later, his work all but done, he said during a slide talk in Minnesota, "It's a long, long preparation for a few moments of innocence."

• • •

Georges Braque admired Cézanne for "sweeping painting clear of the idea of mastery." Such an idea will not stay swept away for long. A new one gradually forms to limit the painter's freedom. By the late sixties with the triumph of American abstract painting mastery had returned. Henry Geldzahler's exhibition, *New York Painting and Sculpture: 1940–1970*, at the Metropolitan Museum of Art could be taken as its apotheosis. Among the reasons to admire Guston is that he picked up Cézanne's broom and swept away this idea of mastery just when painting needed another good housecleaning. This is an act despised by many because it calls into question all that had been thought decided. For others it opens the door to what can be their own art.

Part Three

*Once, years ago, on a panel, Motherwell said he was
searching for the new — the fresh — I couldn't help but
exclaim that "Oh no! I am searching for the old, the lived
through — as though it had been in me for a long
time — a lifetime — but not seen before."*

— PHILIP GUSTON

To Bill, Philip '77.

met Philip Guston in 1972, after a slide show–talk he gave at Boston University. The poet Lewis Warsh, then living in Cambridge, introduced us. Guston had sent Lewis a card telling him of the talk, and Lewis, knowing of my admiration for Guston's work, invited me. We sat with the BU painting and art history students as Guston flashed paintings on the screen and talked through the smoke from his cigarettes. One image, and the exchange that followed, stands out. On a pink ground, more the color of a building in Italy than of the flesh of a white man, three quarters up on the right was a squarish black shape. A window or cloud. Not much to hold your attention. Guston paused to point out that this shape had started all the way over on the left and gradually moved to its present position. Hands shot up. One of the students wanted to know why it stopped where it had. Because, Guston said, that's where it belonged. More hands. His explanation seemed to please no one. The art historians wanted to know more about how he knew the image's proper place, and the painters wanted him to give them an idea of how they could learn the skill of knowing. Guston chuckled and answered that what makes an artist an artist is that he just knows. He left it for all of us to think about the years such knowledge, and trust in it, takes to acquire.

Guston was a hero who became a friend. This had never happened before in my life. I had loved his work on first sight in the midfifties and followed it as best I could despite not living in New York City, but when we met I knew nothing of him as a person. That day in Boston he was fifty-nine and I was thirty. We shook hands outside the lecture hall where he had given the talk. He wanted to know where he could buy a pair of pants as his khakis had a rip in the rear end. I told him, and Lewis and I went off for beers.

33

What I remember most from that first encounter is the intensity of Guston's talk and how serious he was about his art. At the time I was habituated to the sort of irony Americans use to disguise real feeling and still hint at its existence. I say Americans and perhaps this is generally true, but I am referring to the writers and artists I knew at the time. I found Guston's wholehearted absorption in what he was doing a relief and more, an inspiration. In the years I knew him I always awoke the next morning after a late-night talk with the desire to get to work. His commitment to his art was so great that he lifted yours to his level. In his presence there could be no question that making poems matters, and for me this restored my youthful dreams.

I also remember, though this is surely colored by our subsequent friendship, the way he carried himself, a delicate sort of buffalo. Guston was burly but endowed with grace. Or his hands with their long, beautiful fingers lightened and animated his longshoreman's build. At any rate this paradoxical combination had great charm and came to embody for me certain paradoxes in his work. For instance, a lyric touch releasing barbarous images.

What I was then too young to have an inkling about was what young artists mean to older ones. There are ideas and comforts you can get only from your contemporaries, but they will more often than not resent being an audience. If there is the right match, the young artist wants to hear the older artist's story and to sit at his feet and learn. Now that I am fifty I understand how much the older artist wants to tell that story. He need not require sycophancy; Guston didn't. A listener whose interest is genuine and demanding, who is avid for the story but not uncritical makes telling the story more engrossing for the teller. Guston had a great deal to talk about, and I was eager to listen. Our needs made us something like equals, but the truth is that over the years I have come to realize how much separated us. He was on another plane, more thoroughly in his art for longer than I think I have ever been in mine. At the time I was in awe of his devotion, and today I envy the fullness and depth of this because I have known something of it and hope for more.

And I was also impressed by his struggles to both make and establish his art. The us and them battles I had followed as a youth were no longer being fought, and I felt I had missed taking sides in, for example, the beat poets versus the academics. Guston was embattled and heroic because of it. During the years I knew him, his struggles seemed to be part of his art, and they certainly contributed to the legend forming around him. To the viewer who comes to Guston's late work today these battles may mean little. Indeed, one does not have to engage in Guston's struggles to enjoy his art. His beautifully painted ebullient and crude figures are themselves ignorant of the struggles that surrounded them. From the Klansmen onward they are too busy "breeding," Proteus-like in their energy and inventiveness, to be bound by the legend of their creator. His figures had, as Guston knew, a life of their own.

1967–1968

I got sick of all that purity! Wanted to tell stories.
I felt like a movie director, like opening a Pandora's
box and all these images came out.
— PHILIP GUSTON

One day Guston drew, what he came to call "pure drawings." *Air* is lines falling down the paper like rain, *Prague* the bars of a cell high up on the wall of paper, and *Statement* a thick line, also high up, marking the instant of its making. The next day he drew a shoe, a chair, a jalopy, or an open book, common ordinary things. He went back and forth between the pure and the common in what became for him, in his words, "a tug-of-war."

This pull of contradictory impulses began in a general upheaval following his Jewish Museum show. A major show shakes any artist.

Does this mean the end of something? What is next? Blunt questions that only work will answer. But turmoil in Guston's private life kept him from working. He separated from his wife, leaving her for a younger woman, a separation that lasted until he cleared out of his Twentieth Street studio for Woodstock and entered a new studio, on Christmas Day 1967, with both his work and his life still up in the air.

During the woodshedding that followed, a time Guston spoke of as clearing the decks, he did not paint. Painting would resolve the issues, but these were joined, contrary forms vying for his allegiance, in what Guston once referred to as the "barrenness of drawing." In the late forties his abstract work evolved slowly through several transitional paintings. His desire to paint figures simply gave way over time. There was also the sense of abstraction as being both the painting of the time, a cause, and the next step, a natural progression. Now there were two impulses at loggerheads and no strong current in the culture of painting to support or second either impulse. He was on his own.

As Guston drew, he fought the shoes and books that it gave him such pleasure to draw. The pure drawings seemed right, and they had twenty years of his history as a painter to back them up. They came from somewhere he knew. Over his last decade, the shoes having won out, he looked back on this time as transitional, but in the midst of it he had no way of knowing this. He did not know if he was coming or going.

The simplicity and elan of the pure drawings declares assurance, an inevitable rightness. They often look like they made themselves. No fuss or bother — bull's-eye! It is the shoes that have a clunky, used quality. They do not look new but old, odds and ends from some long forgotten closet. The shoes have known a working man's foot, and the books lay flat, like hard-used cookbooks or religious texts read until their spines broke.

If Guston thought he was in search of fresh images these shoes and books must have been perplexing. What was their purpose? The pure drawings could just be. They did not have to express anything but their own sleek existence. Shoes suggest feet. Work boots imply work, workmen or farmers. Books hold words. Could these things simply be? How could they not be fragments of some story? And if they are, what is the story and where does it lead?

Perhaps Guston endured this tug-of-war as long as he did because he enjoyed the contest between the thin art of the pure drawings and the relief he felt in drawing homely, in his words, "tangible things." He always spoke of this time with pleasure. Throughout his art Guston thrived on doubt, but here he was beset by two demanding forces, compelled to follow both to . . . where? Talking with Bill Berkson in 1965 Guston seemed to yearn for such a state: "But I want to find out what happens when you can either not act or not not act. Doubt itself becomes a form. You work to divest yourself of what you know."

We do not know exactly when Guston lost his desire to make another pure drawing nor do we know which overturned shoe or thick boot won the contest. We do know that while in this contest Guston began to want to tell stories, and to use the vocabulary of tangible things as a means to that end. When this impulse could no longer be denied Guston knew he had left abstract painting behind.

A 1969 *Clock* strikes seven. It is the year of the first of the new Ku Klux Klansmen. From here on until the end of his life clocks will tick in Guston's paintings. He knew he was working against time, and he often worked round the clock over the next decade. He also knew that his images were heavy with time and not just art historical time. They had been shaped by the years they had spent in him. He worked like a man starved for objects, hell-bent to enter a world only he could create, anxious to see what he could make happen next. He gave himself first to his Klansmen, born out of the murders of Martin Luther King, Jr. and Robert Kennedy, the rampage of Daley's Chicago cops at the 1968 Democratic National Convention, and quickened by his memory of the hooded figures he had painted in another time of political tumult. A horde of images would follow these Klansmen.

Riding with the Klan

It was difficult for many who first encountered Guston's Klansmen at the 1970 Marlborough show to connect them with current American political realities. Not that Guston ever hid this connection. Indeed, he pointedly addressed the nation's new race consciousness, the Vietnam War, and the rising national lawlessness. Perhaps those who could not see this or refused to had their vision blinkered by the art world. For some sophisticates the Klan paintings were descendants of Pop Art. They read this in Guston's cartoon style and accepted it as evidence that Guston had forsaken twenty years of abstract painting to follow a trend. Since they were adept at spotting quick change artists and keeping up with the style-a-year art world this was only logical. That Guston's Klansmen, emblematic of evil since their first incarnation after the Civil War, might be riding again in Los Angeles, Chicago, and Washington went right by critics and friends who saw these paintings only in terms of art.

It is not that Guston had become an editorial page cartoonist commenting on the passing scene. His Klansmen gain dimension when we take into account the public context in which they emerged, but they have a life independent of this. In painting them Guston drew on deeper associations than the nightly news.

In his drawing, made at age seventeen, for the painting *Conspirators* (another signature image reproduced in every major catalog or book on Guston's work) a hooded figure works to knot a noose out of a hawser-thick length of rope. Behind him six Klansmen plot under a tree from which a lynched black man hangs. The hoods and robes these Klansmen wear are more tailored and refined than those Guston will dress his Klan in nearly forty years later. They resemble the robes of penitents in an Italian Renaissance fresco. His late sixties Klansmen look like their outfits were cut from flour sacks. Their doughlike lumpishness is a world away from the elegance of Guston's first Klansmen.

As Guston drew and painted these conspirators in 1930, the Klan marched between 4 and 5 million knights across America. In his native Los Angeles, Guston watched the Klan parade. Their spectacle impressed him mightily. (Around the same time, in Pennsylvania's northeast corner, my grandfather saw crosses burn on the hilltops surrounding his small town. This impressed him with such force that years later he took me, at age ten, to the places where the burning crosses had stood and told me of the "bad men" who had done such things.)

In reaction to the Scottsboro Boys, Guston painted the murals that were shot up by the marauding Los Angeles Police Department "Red Squad." He spoke of bringing this history to bear when he read the daily papers and watched the news on television throughout the late sixties. With violence epidemic and America's violent streak everywhere apparent and endlessly decried, debated, and denied, Guston felt, as he later explained, "a frustrated fury about everything." He determined not to be what in another context he called "a painting monkey," not to paint stripes, not to turn his raw emotion into "art."

As I write the Klan is with us again. David Duke, a former Klansman, is prominent enough to have run for governor in his home state of Louisiana and, briefly, attempted a run for president of the United States. When Duke removed his hood he revealed a face freshly made over by plastic surgery. His new boy-next-door looks would have delighted Guston as Duke took off one mask to show another. In doing so he mocked himself, but the support he drew (I can see Guston's "what's new?" shrug and hear his chuckle) tells us that the Klan are not the kooks buzzing around the political fringe we like to think they are. While Guston painted his Klansmen the young Duke marched and organized under a robe and hood.

And so, through the years he painted the Klansmen, Guston imagined himself wearing a hood. As his hero Isaac Babel rode with General Budenny's Cossacks into Poland after World War I so Guston imagined himself riding with the Klan. A remarkable feature of these paintings is that Guston is not outside them. They are not images he loftily dispatched into the world to express his dismay and disgust at America. Guston is one with the Klan, an accomplice of sorts. His is a generous and disquieting view, one that includes both artist and observer and with compelling moral urgency lets no one off the hook. In a time of thundering judgments Guston refused that high ground, implying that the human reality of American corruption and political violence is not a simple matter of us and them. His paintings suggest that our intimacy with such violence has had an effect on us that the level of outrage masks or otherwise deflects us from seeing.

We begin to grasp this in *The Studio*. The painter, caught "red handed" with brush poised in his large red mitt as the curtain lifts, is at work on a self-portrait. A bare lightbulb hanging from a cord lights his studio. Similar bulbs hang in the basement hideouts of his fellow hooded conspirators. *The Studio* glows red, pink, white, black, orange, and green. It is a lavishly and lovingly painted image. The paint confers dignity on a figure whose hood is blood spattered (or is it paint?), who is a brother Klansman. This luscious paint slows our look, forcing us to think twice about the relationship of painter to painting. The obvious story this picture tells is that the painter is one with the world he paints. Yet, in pulling up the curtain Guston shows us that this is a painter's world, a world created out of his own needs and desires. We may glimpse these, but in the act of revealing much is withheld.

The Studio does not stop at asking us to ponder the power of illusion in paint. Guston has cast his lot with the smoking, plotting (we see them commit crimes only against themselves) Klansmen. And if he is one of them what of us? But we do not want to answer this. Our instinct is to recoil from these figures, to laugh derisively at their silly costumes and the vanity that seems to inspire the painter in *The Studio* and to rain outrage on their pointy, sheeted heads. Yet as we condemn what is obviously evil can we swear that we will know the face under the hood as evil? It might be the grocer downtown or the high school gym coach. It might be our uncle. In what circumstance could the face be our own? Does the Klansman recognize himself as evil or does the hood keep that knowledge from him?

Ironically, the sheets Klansmen wear draw attention to the fact that they are masked. They are hiding in plain sight. Part of what makes them evil is that we can recognize them yet not know who they are. We see evil and yet must admit that its essential nature is hidden. Perhaps the painter in the studio is after that essence in his self-portrait, but how can he see it if he will not take off his hood?

But what do we have to fear from Guston's schmo-like figures? They are legless, composed of hoods, chests, arms, and hands. They ride around town in roadsters (Guston places them in the thirties, the time when he first became aware of their existence) showing off. You can think of them as "the boys," as Guston sometimes did, three to the front seat of a car, out on a spree and enjoying their own conspiratorship, bragging about the nastiness they will work with the spiked strikebreakers' clubs they carry. When a cop pulls them over one of them begs to differ, raising his cigar to argue a point. He's a real Philadelphia lawyer.

These Klansmen may dream of a cleaver dismembering their enemies, and their cars carry victims tucked in like cordwood, but this does not keep us from laughing mockingly at them. Perhaps we are amused by their self-advertisement. They do not seem to realize that as soon as they don their hoods and costumes they transform themselves into caricatures. This was lost on those who first saw and commented on these paintings. They tended to make much of what Guston took from cartoon techniques without pointing out that he used these to paint figures who had already made themselves into cartoons.

But the Klansmen's clownish camaraderie and the dress up they affect to inspire themselves does not diminish their capacity for evil. Guston connected them with the Watergate burglars who bungled the break-in, while behind them stood men, bunglers in their own right, willing to violate the Constitution at every turn and blandly lie about their acts. In the president's office they were fucking this and fucking that while in public they made nice.

Today we can see a brother Klansman in President Reagan who conspired to trade missiles for hostages, but not in his own mind,

41

where he was busily imagining that he had liberated the death camps at the end of World War II. Under his aegis, Oliver North made sure that the Ayatollah Khomeini celebrated his birthday with a cake baked by Israeli bakers. Once again plotters in the White House shat on the Constitution at will. When this was made public they simply forgot what they had done. Cross-examined for two hours on television Reagan turned aside nearly every question with a wonderfully fuddy-duddy performance of forgetfulness. None of these shenanigans would be foreign to Guston's Klan. You can imagine them lighting up their cigars in admiration of Reagan and his boys.

Guston's Klansmen are ingratiating but bloody minded. Their crime is murder. They cram bodies into their cars, into garbage cans, and throw bodies down cellar holes. Caught, they raise hell protesting their innocence. Of course, Guston painted these pictures during the Vietnam War, images of which were everywhere. Our leaders were still in the "body count" phase of tidying things up and keeping us in the dark. Now they are much better at it. It is unlikely that George Bush will be embarrassed by 100,000 dead Iraqi soldiers stacked like Klansmen's trophies because he did what he could to keep these images from us.

Bloody minded and blood spattered but always dumpily human, these figures do not appear to be motivated by rage. They have not lost their senses. They are organized, and as they drive the outskirts of their city they reason with each other, and we know there will always be reasons for what they do. In the mocking laughter Guston elicits we can come to accept the Klansmen as our own. What they do is what men will do. We laugh to curse them and remove the curse from ourselves.

Babel rode for only a short time with the Cossacks, and Guston did not stay much longer with his Klansmen. He rode with them in what was his second youth, needing to be a bad boy, a plotter against good taste and convention. He called upon their rude energy because it was a match for his own. In his introduction to Babel's collected stories Lionel Trilling tells us that when a Russian Jew wants to call someone a bull in a china shop he can say a Cossack in a succah, a succah being one of the fragile booths or tabernacles in which meals of the harvest succoth are served. How fragile was the tabernacle of art in New York circa 1970 is plain in the derision Guston's Klansmen brought down on themselves and their creator.

Is it any wonder that this target fired back? Politics, of course, went on as usual. Satire of Guston's sort is too refined an art to lay a glove on an American politician. For their part, art writers now speak of the tradition of Goya and Beckmann, but they did not start to until some years after Guston's Klan first rode. Instead they abused art that would, by the end of the decade, be celebrated. Clearly, Guston's Klan did not anticipate this, and some of their "attack" on the art world has been invented by Guston partisans after the fact of this reception. Guston himself turned up the heat on the art world that scorned him. In 1970 he had reason to imagine that that world might welcome an art of political content and raucous energy. This by and large did not happen, and Guston kept throwing the reviews into a metaphorical Venice canal for the rest of his life. He did this, I think, because it was in his nature to dramatize the moment he realized he stood alone, embattled.

This done he could, and did, withdraw from New York for a few more crucial years. When he returned to the art world he came not as a master or honored elder, but as a maverick who might do anything. And he came with open contempt, fueled in part by bitterness over the initial rejection of the Klan pictures, for those who did not have eyes to see what he was up to.

• • •

Magdalena Dabrowski, who curated the Museum of Modern Art's 1988 retrospective of Guston's drawings and wrote the text for its catalog, has this aside about the Klan paintings in her essay: "(One wonders whether he might also have been looking at the work of Zurbarán, with its frequent motif of hooded monks.)"

One wonders, I suppose, if one's head is full of paintings. If one believes painting comes from painting then one is even more likely to wonder, but where does this desire for a pedigree lead? The this-looks-like-that-therefore school of art historical sleuthing turns the artist into he who cannot help repeating the paintings he has seen. Dabrowski's idle notion misses Guston's desire, savage at times, to reclaim painting from those who see it principally in terms of other paintings. This is another tabernacle Guston meant to trample.

Guston and Babel

Comrades let us not fool ourselves: this is a very important right (the right to write badly), and to take it from us is no small thing. Let us give up this right, and may God help us. And if there is no God, let us help ourselves.

— ISAAC BABEL

So Babel spoke, tongue in cheek, to the 1934 Congress of Soviet Writers. In these words Guston heard a contempt identical to that which he felt for art world commissars who ruled out bad painting. Not that Guston desired to paint on velvet or assume bad painting as a style. He sought freedom from the constraints of authorized painting that met conventional expectations. Guston knew that no committee meets to decree such standards, and yet over time the standards emerge, laws are laid down, and bad is identified and ostracized. He insisted on the painter's duty to risk, to violate the norms of his time, and on his right to fail on his own terms.

Conventional . . . standards . . . risk . . . these words mean what we want them to mean, and soon we are in a rhetorical thicket. Those who maintain the conventional invoke it as a standard while deploring the merely conventional. That risk is to be encouraged has become a cliché. Rules are there to be broken and transcended but . . .

What Guston did was paint as if the right Babel spoke of was not a matter for critics or aestheticians to sort out but for paint to insist on, honor, and test. The pigheaded ignorance of his late images and their shocking force was willed.

If we will not go so deeply against the grain that we surprise ourselves and call into question our own aesthetic standards then we deny ourselves a significant resource. When, Guston wanted to know, is a painting ugly, a painting in bad taste a failure? And when is it a way into new territory? And who makes the laws? Is *bad* the word we use to dismiss what we haven't seen before and what is in effect a criticism of our conception of beauty? What is it that so repels us in a bad painting? Is its energy not something we can draw on? Of course this sort of talk could have been just as cheap as any other had not Guston painted the pictures he did. The right to paint or write badly is meaningless unless you exercise it. In his desire to go where he had not gone before Guston vowed to use every resource at hand, those resources declared off-limits to him by the taste of his times most of all.

In Babel, Guston found a soul brother and inspiration. He told the story of his being conceived in Babel's native Odessa, a love child, with such conviction that I was surprised to discover later that it could not possibly have been true. Babel, the supply officer in General Budenny's cavalry regiment, became Guston's model for his own campaign with the Klan: Babel, "eyeglasses on his nose and autumn in his heart," who fought alongside ferocious Cossacks, excited by battle and constantly facing his own divided nature. Babel, who could never be a Cossack and could not be a Jew while he rode with the Cossacks, fit Guston and the paradoxes in his artistic life perfectly.

And so did Babel's prose, with its reliance on fact. Babel claimed to have no imagination. "I have to know," he wrote in a letter, "everything down to the last vein, otherwise I can't write a thing. My motto is authenticity." He marshaled this knowledge in short, driving sentences. Guston loved the quick art with which Babel described the swift and brutal war Budenny's horde waged in Poland.

He loved what Babel put in, and how much he left out for the reader to imagine. Many of Guston's late paintings operate on a similar principle of composition: floorboards you can walk on, a knout's bloody strings, and the night owl's bloodshot eyes. Guston had in mind the brute clarity of his paintings when he quoted Babel's famous "No iron can stab the heart with such force as a period put just at the right place."

Given Guston's passion for baffling, for what is both clear and unfathomable, the stupefying effect of something so ordinary as a period had great appeal. Babel's grotesque sense of humor also appealed to Guston. His tales of Benya Krik, gang leader of Odessa's ghetto, lace sudden violence with wild comedy. Krik's sister carries her mild groom off to their marriage bed as if he were a mouse in her catlike grip. We already know that she has a slight mustache. Guston's who-me? Klansmen, pop-eyed and bewhiskered wobbly heads, and the naked legs stretched up and over ladders have Babel's comic spirit and the pain it brings home.

In his "Reminiscences of Babel" Konstantin Paustovsky recalls Babel saying, "I work like a mule, but I'm not complaining. I choose the forced labor myself. I'm like a galley slave, chained for life to this oar and in love with it, with every detail of it, with the very wood polished by his hands." It is easy to see Guston, obsessed by his late work, stroking beside Babel on that galley bench growing more and more absorbed in the grain of the wooden oar he pulls.

Painting, Smoking, Eating

Walking through his 1974 Boston University show of new paintings Guston stopped me in front of *Painting, Smoking, Eating.* "People come up to me" — he laughed — "and ask what this plate of steak fries is doing on his chest. 'Why,' I say, 'he's hungry.'"

We looked at the heap of thick steak fries and laughed to think that they could have any other meaning. "This painting will hang in the Louvre." Guston's tone was matter of fact. "I'll be dead but you'll see it there." He was not off by much. Today *Painting, Smoking, Eating* hangs in Amsterdam's Stedelijk Museum.

From age seventeen until his death Guston smoked two to three packs of unfiltered Camels every day. Smoked them down to the nub. Smoked them with a flourish that gave smoking the same allure Bogart or Bette Davis gave it. If you smoked you lit up along with Guston. I quit a few years after his death. It would have been harder to do while he lived; all but impossible to sit without smoking across from him through our late-night talks. Guston digging a Camel from its crumpled pack, tilting it up toward the match flame, and exhaling that first puff in deep pleasure was the artist smoking. In his smoke smoking and art, making art and talking about it, were indivisible.

Smoking cigarettes are everywhere in late Gustons. They can be taken as his signature and a self-portrait. In a very late painting a hand holding a wet brush and smoking cigarette reaches to grasp and pull a light's bead chain. The smoke is blood red, a thick column, muscular, industrial, and alive. Guston's Klansmen puff away like chimneys. A smoking cigarette rests on the edge of the table in *Painter's Table* (also in the 1974 BU show), and there beside the book, shoes, and railroad spikes sits an ashtray full of butts emblematic of thoughts thought and a night's work done. In *Smoking* a wide-eyed head, brow scrunched in thought or anxiety, bedcovers up to its chin, a cigarette where its mouth should be, sends puffs of smoke out the medieval arched window above like an Indian message. A similar head ("lima bean" heads Robert Storr named them) smokes and paints in *Painting, Smoking, Eating*.

Guston ate with a dainty ferocity. He was a good cook with a remarkable memory for meals he had eaten and the gift to make talked about food mouthwatering. I can hear him beginning the account of a meal: "You know when you're hungry? I mean you just want some food, a piece of fresh fish, almost anything will do . . ." At his funeral his dealer David McKee remembered Guston's late-night cravings for shrimp or chocolate pinwheels and off they went to find them. It is easy to imagine Guston imagining a plate of steak fries, crisp with a puddle of catsup on top. The fries coming at the end of a long night's painting could be nourishment and reward.

Three of Guston's passions are creamily painted in *Painting, Smoking, Eating*. The light, as in so many late Gustons, comes through the paint as if released from inside. But the skill that achieved this did not come easily to the recumbent painter. He looks as if no display of skill could please him. He is a driven artist. The fries sit uneaten. They do not distract him from the heap of shoes (are they attached to bodies?) he paints. Even in bed he works. Perhaps he has worked intensely for so long that, asleep, he works on in his dreams.

Guston was driven during this time. He often painted around the clock, but the painting tells us more. The painter's hand drips red. Red the color he applies, yes, but the dripping finger recalls the red-handed Klansman painter in *The Studio*. For these painters painting is such a pleasure that being caught red-handed implies the guilt they feel at enjoying themselves so much. The painter's painting in bed is a refusal to stop doing what delights him. If he is awake do not pinch him because he feels like he is in a dream, the painting goes that well. If he is asleep do not wake him from such a glorious dream.

The paint carries the eye with the assurance with which the painter stroked it on to the canvas. His is a physical world beyond thought of painting, smoking, and eating. He knows nothing else but the desire to create a world of shoes. What it takes to achieve this is total awareness. The painter cannot sleep on the job. The dreamer has his eyes open. He is inside an artificial world — the lightbulb gives him light and the pull cord pulls the shade keeping out the morning sun — a world bound by his imagination. He has only to give painting his all.

48

So the painter is driven but with his consent, at his pleasure. Driven to paint a tangible world out of the elements of his life: smoking (which is breath to him), food, and the colored earth of paint. In stunned attention, his painting finger (so intimate is he with his means he no longer needs a brush) carries him along. He has a cigarette to smoke and a meal to eat when he gets hungry.

One of the paradoxes of late Guston is that the voice we hear in his numerous talks, interviews, and statements does not seem to belong to the characters that populate his paintings. Whereas he spoke with care and precision and was obviously a refined, intelligent, and well-read man, his smoking heads are blunt as a knuckle. They do not seem to have a thought in them. They are, I think, the mind emptied of thought and concentrated in action. Work has earned them the bliss of ignorance.

Guston, intellectual that he was, felt the constraints of his mind like straps holding him back. If images came too easily to him he distrusted them. He wanted images that came from beyond his conscious control but that he could recognize, on second and third look, as truly his own. He did not care to resolve this paradox. He delighted in its strangeness and the possibility that it was a sort of trick he was playing on himself.

His bulbous smoking painters indicted, by their crude vitality, the art world Guston saw around him. You cannot imagine these guys keeping to the programs followed by a Jules Olitski or a Kenneth Noland. How could someone with the desires of the painter in *Painting, Smoking, Eating* be interested in, much less aspire to, the sublime? As a painter he is a smoker, an eater, a shoemaker so deeply involved in the pleasure of his work that he does not want to transcend it. Late Gustons are mostly earthbound. This is their way to approach the sublime. The viewer's eye weighs them and carries that weight as the painter's chest carries the steak fries he will soon lift to his mouth and gobble up.

Guston's Nixon

Well, let us be as tenacious as he is,
let's not leave him alone.

— PHILIP GUSTON

Philip Guston and Richard Nixon are exact contemporaries. Both men grew up in Southern California and came east to fame; both knew great acclaim and rejection, and for both 1966 to 1970 were watershed years during which they forged new careers.

It is likely that Richard Nixon never heard of Guston much less saw one of his paintings. For Guston, Nixon was the American politician of his maturity. Kennedy and Johnson were bit players when compared with the veteran of the Alger Hiss investigation, the Checkers speech, the failed candidate for president who lost by a five o'clock shadow, and the ill-tempered loser for governor of California who dusted himself off and got back in the race. The New Nixon triumphed only to fall with the self-exonerating piety "I am not a crook" on his lips. Nixon embodied the no-holds-barred ambition and bald-faced hypocrisy in American politicians and political life that so amused and galled Guston.

In the early seventies an indignant Guston drew a biography of Nixon's life and political times emphasizing his first presidential administration. Gathering them to make a book, Guston titled the drawings *Alas, Poor Richard.* Hogarth, Goya, and Daumier can be cited as precursors, but none of the three sustained the attention to one career, one personality that Guston's drawings do. *Alas, Poor Richard* begins in Nixon's boyhood Whittier, California, room and ends with the swollen-legged, phlebitis-afflicted "victim" of Watergate limping toward his sunset retreat in Key Biscayne, Florida, where his friend Bebe Rebozo will tend his wounds. As Nixon was a subject Guston and I could never exhaust in talk Guston loaned me a Xerox of the book, and I urged him to exhibit the drawings and find a publisher.

Despite my encouragement Guston could never do more than explore the idea in his characteristically maddening back and forth way. In the end he took back the Xerox copy, adamant in his decision not to publish or show the drawings. He feared the published drawings would be news, *Newsweek* and *Time* news, that could only take attention away from his current paintings. And he feared that if his caricatures drew attention to his paintings it would be to their cartoonlike aspects, further distorting that element to obscure the paintings as a whole. Guston thought *Alas, Poor Richard* would cast him as Mort Sahl with a pen, just another Nixon hater driven to extremes. He had no use for such notoriety. That was seventeen years ago. To date only four of these drawings have been published.

Guston had long been able to "get" his art world friends with his quick-witted pen. In Dore Ashton's *Yes, but . . .* and Robert Storr's *Philip Guston* you can see a baby-faced Robert Motherwell curled in on himself in total self-absorption; "Bill de K," in watch cap, arms folded across his chest like a tough guy casing the joint; Franz Kline is a wedge holding a glass and looks like a suave badger; Harold Rosenberg is all bristly crew cut, eyebrows, and mustache fierceness; and John Cage has an elongated head of expressive plasticity. These date from the fifties and show the caricaturist's unforgiving eye.

Guston imagined Nixon from Quaker cradle to China, anticipating Nixon's actual visit, to exile in Key Biscayne, and then into the

THE RICHARD NIXON STORY

Some days so small, sad
alone and aggressive in splendid misery —
you can write anything
you want about Richard Nixon
but you can't say he ever had a headache.
Untroubled as any glorious
blue sky in the country
those clouds you see
are boredom, ambition and hunger.
This is before lunch.
Those are his three horsemen.
He'll sit down to some
cottage cheese and catsup
discovering the same things
over again

old honorable virtues.
It must be protein
put the smile on Pat's face
a chisel couldn't interrupt
or is it the memory
of those Whittier dates
kind Richard, dogged Richard
drove her home from
when she'd been out
with someone else.
Never in the world imagining
this quiet, can't take a hint
poor, patient Quaker's son
would one day be President
of the world's greatest nation.
And for his part he hummed
along with the car radio
not about to push himself
Certain she will fall
to his plans and devotion
when the time is ripe
Content to be Richard
the faithful
never for the moment
imagining his place in the history
of that great country
he would so soon serve in war.
In the car not even a breath
of the hard work, drudgery really,
handshakes, neglect, applause and insults.
The man who will never
leave well enough alone
and his wife
those fabulous stupors to come
beyond their wildest dreams.

setting sun of San Clemente. Like editorial page cartoonists since Nixon's debut in the forties, Guston had his ski-jump nose and stubbled jowls to work with, but unlike Herblock, Mauldin, and others, Guston was not bound by the decorum of a family newspaper. He could, and did, go too far Pinocchioizing Nixon's nose into a large, sloping prick and puffing out Nixon's blowhard's cheeks to form balls. Nasty fun, and to those of us who share Guston's loathing of Nixon, on the money.

In drawing his art colleagues, Guston had the advantage of friendship and the nerve to use it. His intimacy with Nixon is of a different sort. Guston knew him the way common experience allows us to know others of our own generation. And as a painter, Jew, and leftist, Guston knew his opposite politician, Quaker, Republican, Nixon.

Nixon's improbable 1968 comeback victory certainly got Guston's attention. While Nixon rode the nation's angry turmoil using a handpicked blunt instrument, Spiro T. Agnew, to smash blacks, war protesters, and sundry "nattering nabobs of negativism," Guston, assailed by the Vietnam War and registering the nation's tremors, fed his fears and anger into the Klan paintings. While in railing against crime Nixon slipped on the racist's hood, Guston painted conspirators, Klansmen, plotting evil for evil's sake. *Alas, Poor Richard* scores the "poor" Nixon who from the Checkers speech to Watergate shamelessly peddled himself as a victim. He is the American vulgarian supreme who sweeps aside all rules except those he holds you to, who is never responsible for his fate, and who, when caught out, cries crocodile tears and spitefully pleads that it is you who are unworthy of him. In farewell, he invokes his dear dead mother!

Guston's Nixon is "Tricky Dick" with the cunning turned to full blast. He leers and smirks, and his slitty eyes are always keen for the main chance. During the China visit Guston imagined Nixon speaking Chinese to John Mitchell, a lump of barely comprehending gristle, and Agnew, who is a sublime creation. His head is a doughy pyramid with sparse hair on its pointy crown. Stubblelike nails have been hammered into the back of his neck. He is a feel-good, feel-nothing tourist dressed in a Hawaiian shirt reminding us that one of Agnew's strengths as a vice presidential candidate was that he dressed well. He understands not a word of the Chinese his leader speaks. No problem for Nixon to lord it over such henchmen!

Another sublime creation is Henry Kissinger. The quintessential intellectual in politics, he is his thick black-rimmed glasses scuttling after Nixon. Behind this creepy, crawly, slithering Kissinger there is nothing. He is all vision and no humanity.

Each new Watergate revelation and fresh Nixon attempt to stonewall and cover his ass delighted Guston. The Nixon he drew for my "The Richard Nixon Story" and revived for his painting *San Clemente* shows the president trudging into the sunset, dragging his leg, like his past, behind him, eager for our pity yet turning it away at the same time so we feel awful at the sight of his misery. Awful, as his hope is, yet admiring of his martyrdom. These are Guston's valedictions to the man he continued to follow chortling as news of his visit to Billy Graham, during which Guston imagined Nixon brown-nosing the cross, slipped to the "shipping pages."

Even if the Nixon drawings are but a fascinating sidetrack off Guston's late work, they have a rich message. His Nixon incarnates American contempt for any belief that does not aid self-advancement. Profess anything; believe nothing.

Guston's Nixon is a grifter, craven but indomitable, who learns to make himself the butt of his own jokes, who limps off to lick his wounds crying more for our benefit than over his own pain. He knows he will be back. This Nixon's life of setbacks and triumphs is animated by a wild streak of vulgarity American to the core. Mark Twain is its poet. Guston had the wit and courage in these drawings as he did throughout the work of his last decade to be true to this vulgarity.

The Victim

My God, did I do that?
I can't shake off a nervousness
and melancholy — must be the sign
of renewed paintings coming. You'd
think I'd be used to it by now, but
guess I'm still a victim.
— Philip Guston

Guston often characterized himself as a victim, willingly at the mercy of images that came from out of the blue as he painted through the night. Reentering the studio he could be thrown for a loop, shocked by what he had done. When younger he scraped off these disquieting images. He explained that he could not accept them. Now he hoped for their appearance. In early October of 1975, as he began the semester at Boston University, we met for lunch at the Union Oyster House on Stuart Street. Ladies out shopping crowded the place. As we ate Guston talked excitedly of his summer's run of painting. He was really wound up. As our voices rose the ladies stole looks over their shoulders at us. If Guston noticed he ignored them, and we sat on over drinks as he talked and traced his new paintings in the air. Guston's long expressive fingers mimed his paintings as he spoke. He had the gift of using his hands to help you see, and that afternoon he drew in the air a stretch of barren land into which legs had come.

He was possessed by the leg paintings, "clumps of legs," as he described them, over twenty of which he had completed that summer. He had no idea where the image originated. Legs, bare, shod legs, bent at the knee, *L*-shaped legs knotted or held together like . . . what? Like the wet, writhing clump of night crawlers my grandfather lifted from his worm box to drop into his bait can as he prepared to go fishing? That's the first image I came up with. As Guston continued his description it was the legs' arrival more than what they looked like, and the absolute command to paint them and the trust he had in what he was doing that perplexed and possessed him.

He did connect the legs with a recent interest in the Michelangelo frescoes next to the Sistine Chapel. The barren ground or no-man's-land on which Michelangelo set the dramatic action of the crucifixion of Saint Peter and Saint Paul caused him to see that any action set in such a wasteland would be dramatic. He put the legs in *Monument* on that same greenish, featureless ground. At the time I did not know the Michelangelo frescoes, so I looked them up at once. I could see the pitiless power of the steppelike landscape. I also saw, since legs were on my mind, the many legs of horses in the frescoes and the raised-leg, stamping motion of a few of the horses.

Although I could usually see Philip's new work as he outlined it in talk, the leg paintings eluded me. I could not separate legs from torso and could not imagine legs free from a body yet joined together. The image struck me as ludicrous, at least the gummy ball of spaghetti image that formed in my mind did. When I finally saw *Monument, Rug, Green Rugs*, and others in the series I was stymied. They were terrible and fascinating in their weirdness, but I did not know what to make of them. If I laughed at them it was an ill-at-ease laugh out of not knowing how else to respond. They made me uncomfortable, *Monument* especially, as if I had come across something totally human yet coldly uncommunicative, an Ozymandias whose existence I could not account for and whose expression I had no hope of reading.

I still cannot fathom these paintings. To me they are images of anxiety and annihilation or of an anxiety that feels like annihilation. They project an obdurate, unexplainable, arrogant, and totally indifferent force. Their soul seems an absence of soul. Look closely and they are as beautifully painted as other late Gustons. You can get lost in and be lifted by this paint, but step back, feel their onslaught, and it is difficult, perhaps impossible, to warm to them. These legs are Guston's most powerful statement against the desire to be loved, the beseeching call for sympathy he decried in so much of the art of his times.

I did make one connection with the legs, and it was literary. Shortly before seeing *Monument* I had read Joseph Conrad's "Typhoon." In it a merchant ship carrying a cargo of Chinese coolies is pitched and tossed by a typhoon. As I studied Guston's painting, a vision of these men, thrown together, entangled, frightened out of their wits, a mess of limbs rose to mind.

Monument is a loud painting; I thought so that day I first saw it at David McKee's gallery, and I still think so. The feet are iron shod, and they stomp like folk dancers or marching soldiers. Between the legs you can see for some distance. They could have come a great way over the barren plain. The legs are pink and red with exertion. The title says they have done their traveling and are here for good. But a monument to what? Perhaps to the powerful force inherent in things we recognize but do not understand. We know they are legs, but have no idea what they represent. Guston has put us in the position of a late-eighteenth-century traveler coming upon ruins in the Egyptian desert. What sort of civilization might we imagine from this monument of legs?

In *Rug* the tangle of legs stomps in from stage right like demented Rockettes doing a burlesque number. Legs burst through *The Door* feet first. It is numbered 660, Guston's street address, like a hotel room door. Invited guests? Not on your life. In *The Street* legs face off against paws thrusting garbage can lid shields in a parody of heroic sculpture. Legs crawl, stretched painfully, over a brick wall in *Ancient Wall.*

Green Rug, which Guston thought enough of to have as the cover image of his 1980 retrospective catalog, shows only two legs, but they are disconcerting nonetheless. The painting's background is dead-of-night black. The legs in nailed shoe soles dance on a green fringed rug as do the shadows of the soles. The rug is on a wood floor, which does nothing to assure the viewer that he is in fact looking into a room. This floor could be over an abyss. To the right, high up and floating, is a knout with six blood red strings. Is it there as a symbol of discipline to keep the legs in line? Or is it about to flay the legs and make them dance with pain? Whips abound in late Gustons. Klansmen use them on one another like medieval scourges. Several of the smoking painters wield whiplike brushes. Beside the open 660 door, where some homes have a hat rack, a knout hangs from a nail, ready at hand. These Cossack knouts, sailors' cat-o'-nine-tails, penitents' scourges imply that the painter whips his images, tames them, fixes them in paint as he is whipped to do so by them. Letting images come, letting the brush have the whip hand is a painful process, and the painter is doubly a victim, first of the unbidden images themselves and then of their insistence to be seen.

Entrance, from 1978, depicts legs pushing through a studio door escorted by a guard of bugs. These emerge from a storm of paint, a nightmare of decisions and indecisions, through which the painter brought them to life. Or he could no longer resist them, and their creator is their victim. Painting is an act of submission. If you truly must have your own way; if you are determined to see what is behind the door, what you know to be there but have yet to see then you will be dominated by what this desire produces.

The poet Jack Spicer said, "Poets think they are pitchers, but they're really catchers." *Entrance,* all the leg paintings, made Guston a catcher, for him a hoped for, a striven for position. To get there you must stop thinking you know what is behind the door. You come to it by letting it come to you. A certain ignorance — the catcher wears "the tools of ignorance" — needs to be cultivated. If you know too much you will not be ready for anything. And you cannot be too rational. The rational man finds it impossible to believe that anything can happen. We tend to think of inspiration as exalting, a bolt from the blue in which illuminating instant we see and act with unusual clarity and certainty. Not in Guston's studio. In several conversations he described his mental state there as "delirium," and the legs as its product and emblem. Emerson thought that any poem could be saved by one "wild cry from the heart." To hear this cry and write it you must, the leg paintings tell me, surrender to it. Forty years as a painter provided Guston with the means to let himself become the victim of his imagination.

Guston's Jewishness

That Philip Guston was Philip Goldstein's creation has caused speculation that Goldstein, fearing anti-Semitism or out of self-hatred, chose to hide his Jewishness. Certainly, as a child Goldstein heard of the pogroms that had forced his family to flee their native Odessa. And by the time he began using Guston at twenty-two he must have known anti-Semitism firsthand. The Guston I knew never hid his Jewishness nor did he reveal to me his name change. I felt a slight shock when I read of it in his daughter Musa Mayer's book *Night Studio*.

His daughter writes that Guston required Dore Ashton not to mention the change in her 1976 book *Yes, but* . . . . Mayer also remembers a family story claiming Guston changed the name for fear his wife's parents might object to his marrying their daughter. Mayer herself was ignorant of the change until college. Growing up she saw her father's mother only once and had no contact with the family in Los Angeles. In writing her book she sought out her father's cousin and asked her about the name change. "We felt," the cousin explained, "as an artist that's what he needed to do — nobody questioned it. When you get into that business — well, it's like show business."

After deriving Guston from Goldstein he did not impulsively take up the new name. Out of lifelong intellectual habit a "Yes, but . . ." debate must have taken place. He used the name off and on for two years, trying it on for fit, before at twenty-four and newly married he made the change official. Guston was not only newly wed but freshly arrived in New York. He may have felt like an immigrant and reasoned that his new status and home entitled him to a new name. But as the pledge he exacted from Ashton suggests, he never got over a feeling of shame. His daughter quotes an autobiographical fragment written in 1980, the year of his death, in which he set down a persistent desire, thwarted as he looks back, to escape his Goldstein family. While Goldstein is a common Jewish name, Guston is unusual if not one of a kind and announces no clear ethnic background. The name puffs out; it has a barrel chest, a swagger. If you are in the process of inventing yourself as a painter why not take a name with a confident ring to it? If one of Guston's motives was to adopt a memorable "stage" name it is also possible that he wanted not to be the son of his suicide father.

As far as is known anti-Semitism played no part in Leib Goldstein's suicide nor in what little we know of the failures that reduced him from railroad mechanic to junk man crying "Rags and old iron!" through the Los Angeles streets. Guston spoke to me only once about his father's death. It was the last evening we spent together. We were at a breakup dinner for his BU classes, and we sat at a table of graduate students eager for his attentions. Guston turned away from them and recited to me, as if under indictment, how he came home from school to discover his father and, with a kitchen knife, cut through the rope "thick as a hawser" (as I type them I can hear him say the words) to let his dead father down. I did not believe him. Despite the conviction in Guston's voice something I cannot put my finger on to this day prompted this reaction. Perhaps the story came out so perfectly it sounded rehearsed. Perhaps I heard in it his fears of his own death that had arisen from his recent heart attack. At any rate the desperate rush in which he told the story and my own intuition about it spooked me.

It was not until Robert Storr interviewed me for his book on Guston that I learned Lewis Goldstein had hanged himself when Guston was seven. It is difficult to credit a child of that age taking down a hanging grown man, but whatever actually happened it is not surprising that his father's death remained with Guston and came to him again with such vividness so near his own.

In giving up his father's name Guston did not reject his Jewishness, and the late work is testimony to this. As he began the Klan paintings he followed the example of Isaac Babel, Jew and Cossack. Like Babel, Guston stood apart from his tribe and like him also was a witness, an anxious one, aware that at any moment he could become a victim. Babel and Guston gorged their imaginations on violent images, images that mirrored their conflicted natures. Both artists were unsparing and apologetic in their pursuit of violence. They knew for a moral certainty that men desire violence more than they desire peace and that our violent acts give truthful expression to who we really are.

As Babel wandered with the Cossacks through the villages of Poland, Guston wandered with his Klan. When I look at the shoes and boots Guston constantly painted with such loving attention to their worn, lived-in homeliness, I think of van Gogh's farmers' and miners' boots, but mostly I think of wandering. We work with our hands: we think on our feet and then kick off our shoes and go to bed. When thinking, we pace, and we go for walks to clear our heads. The shoe is directly connected to the mind, and to wandering, through which we carry our identity in our minds. No tribe has wandered like the Jews have. Something of their tale is told again in the handmade stoutness and humorous goodwill of Guston's shoes and boots. They will serve to carry you along no matter how many the miles to go.

The Coat II image on the 1980 retrospective poster lugs shoes under its arms as does the coated figure in *Back View*. Both figures cross a red ground or sea emerging from and heading toward weather or emptiness without reference to place. They are monoliths of travel, eternal immigrants, dressed in coats of thick tweed, buttoned up like the one coat you would choose to wear when leaving home for good. The shoes these figures carry may be spares for the long journey. Or they are the shod feet of those ancestors we drag behind us, our history and identity. Shod legs stick up out of *Cellar*, stick up as if sown like corn in *Ominous Land,* and in *Dawn,* legs are stacked in a Klansman's jalopy. They could be the legs of Auschwitz corpses. Bodiless legs are anonymous; human refuse stacked like logs. These victims of the Klan's dirty work are as anonymous as the death camp dead. As these legs call to mind the death camps, Guston's books call up images of the libraries in the rebbe's courts Roman Vishniac photographed in pre-World War II Warsaw. There behatted men and boys, soon to be annihilated, sat buried (what a word!) in their tattered, dog-eared precious texts. Guston's books speak of the absolute dedication of these students and remind us how otherworldly it is to have your nose in a book, to be lost in study or reading. "I read a lot so there are books around the house, and it's natural for me to draw and paint them." Guston may not have used these exact words, but he said similar things in response to the numbingly obvious questions he kept on being asked after 1970. How odd that so many open books could be thought to have a hidden purpose. Then again it must be that all books are in hiding and reveal their designs only over time. Guston's books might be dictionaries or cookbooks, any books whose spine we bend and crack to our purpose. They also look like books in which we might encounter our fate. Guston put such heft in them that it is possible to believe that what we take from them is physical. These books, Guston loved to quote Kafka, could "serve as an ax for the frozen sea within us."

Books, stacked shod legs, shoes, Kafka, Babel, and Jewishness — these can seem to make a straight line of conscious intent there for all to see. But Guston, who loved to talk about his work, whose talk about his late work is part of that work, never drew this line. Perhaps he thought it so obvious it needed no comment from him. Perhaps the obvious never occurred to him. Perhaps when you traffic in images of such dailiness, of such intimate personal use it is impossible to control or even conceive of all the stories these images tell. You have let loose more than you can ever know. Guston knew his late paintings were after what had been in him a long time, images that he had to go deep for, images that he could not describe before the fact of their making but would recognize. Images that

63

were his and his alone. The Jewishness he masked in naming himself Guston is one such old and intimate presence he pulled up from the
deepening well of his liberated imagination.

• • •

At Guston's funeral a rabbi gave the Prayer for the Dead, *El Mole
Rachamim.* Amid the Hebrew song, "Philip Guston" rang out like a
declaration and pierced like a bird's cry. That day Guston's ashes
were buried with a few paintbrushes and a tube of cadmium red
medium, his color.

"The Kind of Paintings
You Like"

During the years I knew Guston he taught graduate students at
Boston University. This required him to be in Boston three or
four days each month during the academic year. He took the job
because he needed the money. He had, he said, "a nest egg," but his
paintings were not selling. I remember that out of one New York
show he sold only a single drawing to Jasper Johns. Guston also took
the job because he needed to get away from the studio and talk. For
all the unwelcome distractions BU brought, his visits allowed him to
come up for air.

Most months he called when he arrived in town and made a date
for dinner. He loved food, and it was a pleasure to see the pleasure he
took in eating. The meal did not have to be grand, broiled swordfish
or a dish of pasta did the trick. He talked as he ate. Usually, the work
he had just left was on his mind, and this, as always, he sketched in
the air with his active, eloquent hands. I loved to hear his excited
talk of new work. I never failed to draw from him energy that sparked

my own writing. And I loved to get him talking about the fifties in New York.

Max Beerbohm was right when he wrote, "It is the period that we didn't quite know, the period just before oneself, the period of which the earliest days one knew the actual survivors, that lays a really strong hold on one's heart." I was in precisely that relationship to the Cedar Bar, The Club, to Kline, de Kooning, and Pollock. I wanted to know as much as I could about those times and the heroes whose work triggered my own first interest in art.

As forthcoming as Guston was when I nudged him in that direction, he made it clear he did not want to dwell on those days. He had little use for nostalgia, and he did not want his current work obscured by any good-old-days fog. Yet he told a good story. I remember his account of de Kooning's putting down the musician and collector Ben Heller at a party in Heller's penthouse. Heller began to lecture a crowd of painters about Goya. Soon de Kooning had had all he could stand. No one, he shouted, can talk about Goya but a painter, but me! Meanwhile Franz Kline slipped a bottle of Heller's best Scotch into the pocket of the raincoat he always wore. Upon getting the high sign from Kline, the painters bid farewell and met in a nearby bar to whoop it up on Kline's theft, toasting de Kooning's outburst.

After dinner Guston and I sat talking and smoking Camels and drinking, beer or wine for me, and a little Scotch in milk for him, until midnight and often into the wee hours. Since his death it is these unfettered talks I have missed. One subject was linked to the next, forming an unbroken chain of conversation. No subject was out of bounds. We were nitpickers one minute and laughing the next. As I have grown older I have felt the loss of those admired elders I can now no longer listen to and talk with. "All the Olympians; a thing never known again," as Yeats says in his poem "Beautiful Lofty Things."

One night I asked had he ever exchanged paintings with any of his friends in those days. No, he answered, but he came close once with Kline. They were in Chicago for a two-man show in the late fifties. Instead of an opening dinner the dealer gave them a hundred bucks and with a pat on the back sent them off for a night on the town, "two visiting firemen." They ate a good dinner and then strolled past the strip joints on Rush Street. A barker, marking them as two rubes, grabbed Kline's arm and waved them inside with a stage whisper promising, "Fresh cunts from Cincinnati."

This broke them up, buoyed their night, and they went on a drinking spree. In their cups, one or the other of them, Guston had forgotten who, said they really ought to trade pictures. They agreed enthusiastically and shook hands on the deal. But hungover the next morning neither one mentioned the agreement, and they never spoke of it again.

These stories were set pieces. On other nights, in response to questions, he spoke of de Kooning, whom he kept in touch with by phone, his admiration for him and how much he and other painters were influenced by *Excavation*. He spoke of Morton Feldman and John Cage, but never of their music. And he never said a thing about Pollock. It was like pulling teeth to get him to talk about his own paintings of the fifties. "The kind of paintings" — he snorted in proud contempt and jerked a thumb in my direction — "you like." Proud because they were his, and he knew their quality. Contempt because he did not want them put on the same plane as his new work. The fifties paintings made him squirm a little. He was no longer that painter and did not want to, even for a moment, get back into work that he felt bound him like a straitjacket.

By the early seventies abstract painting oppressed him. He saw it in every airport and public building. What had been a breakthrough for him and then "a beautiful land" was now visual Esperanto designed in Cape Town, Singapore, Moscow, and St. Louis. He saw that the appeal of abstraction was that it could mean anything. Since it lacked subject matter it could be used for decoration internationally. He knew his old work was of a different and higher quality than this, but he dismissed it as needing too much, in his word, "sympathy." He saw those who extolled fifties abstract painting as a club of art lovers eager to accept the painting on any terms. This sickened him.

66

Guston pushed away such sympathy with both hands. He instinctively mistrusted any understanding of his work, any formulation that encouraged the viewer to get chummy with his pictures. Guston detested the consensus that endorsed abstraction. The world now seemed to know for certain what art was, but he was not so sure he did. Guston lived perpetually in the six weeks Morton Feldman remembered from the fifties. "What was so great," Feldman wrote, "about the fifties is that for one brief moment — maybe, say, six weeks — nobody understood art."

When Guston evolved out of abstract painting he left, as John Cage lamented, "a beautiful land." Guston acknowledged this, but he knew he no longer wanted beauty on those terms. Not under the art lovers' seal of approval. He could only begin his late work by abandoning what he had done. This was both a reprise of what happened in the late forties and something entirely new.

In the late forties the wave of abstract painting began to build. De Kooning, Kline, and, especially, Pollock were in full surge. Guston, no matter what his struggles, looked like a convert who was determined to catch the crest of the wave. No one could have had such a thought at his 1970 Marlborough show. Save for de Kooning, the great first-generation abstract painters were dead and safely enshrined. Fortune left Guston without contemporaries. There was little to measure his work against except the work of de Kooning and the finished work of Pollock, Kline, and Rothko. Few gave a thought to what Kline might have done had he lived into his sixties. Had he lived might Pollock have returned to images like *She-Wolf,* and might Rothko have picked up the surrealist thread he let drop?

And so Guston felt under the shadow of his abstractions and the even heavier shadow of abstract painting's heroic dream. He did not want his late work to be held hostage by the fifties. He had to establish new terms. This put an edge on his unwillingness to discuss his abstract paintings. He had left one land for another, and he was determined not to let his past stand in judgment over his future. Those who expressed bitterness at what they believed to be Guston's betrayal of his gifts and principles deepened and then confirmed his contempt for the art world rigidities, the chapter and verse, that had grown up around abstract painting.

As the seventies progressed, Guston believed that he had been wrong in the fifties and was now in the right. It was a matter of life and death. Perhaps anyone who thinks in such extremes invites the worm of doubt. Ross Feld told me the following story. In the late seventies he and Guston had just come from a show of the painter James Brooks's new work. A friend of Guston's since the thirties, Brooks painted abstractions all his life. Feld and Guston were on Madison Avenue heading uptown. Neither spoke a word until Guston stopped, turned to Feld, and exclaimed in anguish, "Maybe he's right and I'm wrong!"

Acceptance, early and late, troubled Guston. He could stand it only so long before recoiling from it. When *Life* wrote about him in 1946 he dismissed his prize-winning painting *Sentimental Moment* as "too literal." During the fifties it disturbed him that painters influenced by his work picked up only the work's most obvious aspects, for instance that he did not paint all the way to the frame. At the same time he hated the attacks and indifference that met his late works. Nothing, no reception, satisfied him because his painting could never be contained in what others thought of it. He battered down every certainty, his own first of all. He was in a perpetual state of saying yes and then no, and out of this quarrel with himself came the energy that produced much of his art. At times our evening talks dissolved into something like acid. There seemed no answer to "And then what do we want?" except to go to bed and hope to wake from the bad dream of stale alternatives. I always did wake the next morning with the faith that what resolution there might be could only honorably be found in work. I came to see this as a lesson I learned from Guston about how to be an artist.

Reading Poets

*These past couple of weeks has been poems — drawings
instead of painting — When I get the call — is the best way
of doing them of course. A sort of immersion in poetry.*

— PHILIP GUSTON

The Museum of Modern Art's 1986 drawing retrospective failed
on two counts to present the full range of Guston's drawings.
None of his caricatures appeared nor did a single example of his
many drawings of poems. These were probably left out in favor of

"major" drawings. Whatever the curator's high-mindedness, their absence robbed viewers of an aspect of Guston's work that gave him great pleasure.

Guston's wife, Musa, was a poet of wit and originality, whose modesty kept her from publishing widely. Guston did numerous drawings of her work for her pleasure as well as his own. I say "of" because he did not illustrate or collaborate except in the case of Clark Coolidge. Guston read the poems with his pen, wrote them out word for word and let the images and connections thus inspired come through.

The Coolidge-Guston drawings ("exchange" is Coolidge's word for them) are different because image begat word and word image. They provoked one another to see what might come of it. The drawings for Bill Berkson's *Enigma Variations* are the closest Guston came to illustration. Berkson's book is a selected poems for which Guston provided drawings, abstract and figurative, from the years the poems were written.

In my case Guston drew thirteen poems. I had no idea he was doing this. Because he had agreed to do the cover for *Columbus Square Journal* he had the manuscript. Incidentally, he gave the book its title. The manuscript bore the title *Columbus Day a Year*. It displeased my ear, but I could come up with nothing better. Ignoring this title Guston simply called the book a journal, which it is, and named it after my address. The image under this name, a brick wall surmounted by a drawn shade, appeared three years later in his painting *Smoke*.

After he made the cover he did the drawings of my poems. One night Guston came to dinner carrying a large portfolio from which, to my surprised delight, he took drawings of a dozen poems from the journal and the drawing of "The Richard Nixon Story." I have no idea why he chose these poems other than that they inspired him. I do know that at least one of the drawings predates his having my manuscript. A photograph in Dore Ashton's book shows it hanging on his studio wall. He must have thought of it when he read my poem, an elegy to Walker Evans, and lettered in the poem.

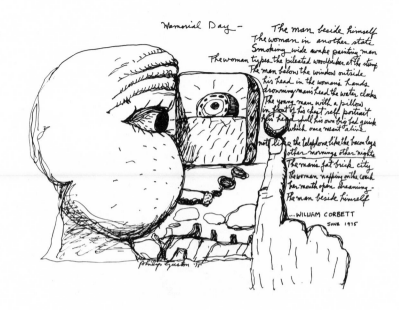

The man beside himself
The woman in another state
Smoking wide awake paint man
The woman types the pileated woodpecker at the stump
The man below the window outside
his head in the woman's hands
drowning man's head the water clocks.
The young man with a pillow
in front of his chest self portrait
his head full his own big bed quick
which once meant alive
not like the telephone like the bacon legs
other mornings other nights
The man's fat brick city
The woman napping on the couch
her mouth open dreaming
The man beside himself

— WILLIAM CORBETT

Each drawing emphasized some aspect of the poem that I now saw in a fresh way. The Nixon, for example, has Nixon caterwauling. I meant to have Nixon feeling sorry for himself, and this is what the huge tears do, but in a more vivid way than my words hinted at. Guston took the poem a step (the pun is unavoidable) further by picturing Nixon with his phlebitis-swollen leg at his retreat in Key Biscayne, Florida. Neither illness nor vacation home is in my poem.

And the genius touch of the garter correctly holding up the sock on Nixon's elephantine leg is pure Guston. After all, Nixon is from the Tom Dewey wing of the GOP and has often been pictured relaxing at home in a business suit.

Throughout the years of his late work, Guston enjoyed and sought out the company of writers. Philip Roth was a neighbor and friend

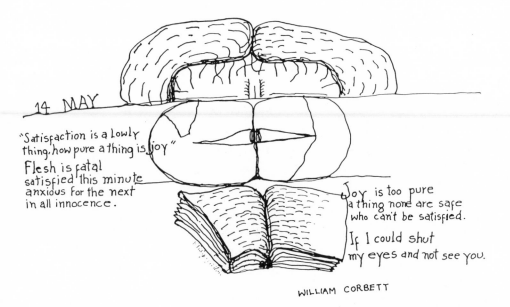

14 MAY

"Satisfaction is a lowly
thing. how pure a thing is joy"

Flesh is fatal
satisfied this minute
anxious for the next
in all innocence.

Joy is too pure
a thing none are safe
who can't be satisfied.

If I could shut
my eyes and not see you.

WILLIAM CORBETT

in the late sixties and early seventies. Imagine the conversations they must have had about Nixon! Ross Feld wrote what Guston thought was an uncommonly perceptive review, and Guston got in touch with him, initiating an important friendship. "The few people who visit," Guston said, "are poets or writers rather than painters because I value their reactions. Looking at this painting (*Painter's Forms*), Clark Coolidge, a poet who lives thirty miles away, said that it looked as if an invisible presence had been there, but had left these objects and gone somewhere else. I like that kind of reaction, compared with reactions like 'the green works, the blue doesn't work.'" Guston, well read in philosophy, art history, and poetry, spoke of "reading" paintings, and perhaps this habit drew him to writers who read his paintings and discovered stories in them.

His late works certainly opened the word-hoard and drew language from me. These pictures inspire talk, and not just, not even primarily, art talk. The cars Guston's Klansmen scoot around the outskirts of town in are roadsters, runabouts, and jalopies. The legs in the leg paintings stomp, clomp, parade like snarled soldiers and put their feet to the floor like savage dancers. They make a noise somewhere between a thump and a clatter. His painters, grizzled as Gabby Hayes, look like death warmed over.

Guston's forms incite words and invigorate the common phrase. He depicted these painter's forms popping out of an open mouth. They summon their own names and call for an account of their actions. You can, in looking at late Gustons, join his story, build on it and keep it going. You want — this writer emphatically does — to enjoy the physical pleasure of getting a word and more around Guston's images. Part of the charge these paintings give comes when their content inevitably loosens the tongue.

A Visit to Woodstock

Beverly and I drove out from Boston on a May Friday expecting to spend the weekend at the Gustons'. Philip had urged us to come and see what he called their "digs." We found the house on Maverick Road with no trouble. Philip had propped a hand-painted GUSTON sign on the mailbox.

Then as now the house is hidden from the road by bushes. Next to it, built of cinder block, the studio could be taken for a small factory. Nothing suggests its real purpose. Across the road, woods rise up a steep, rocky hill. The Gustons' one-story shingled bungalow stood pleasantly isolated from their neighbors.

Inside the house was shipshape and snug, comfortable and unpretentious. Only Philip's art on the walls. I remember a few paintings from the late fifties in the living room. Given his ambivalence about this work, these surprised me. But then he knew the quality of his specific works even as he rejected the sort of painting they represented. A picture window looked out toward the back of their property, where a stone potter's studio built by a former owner stood. Philip had once used this as a studio, but now Musa worked there. When we were given a look inside we saw groups of birds' nests, stones, and seashells, the sorts of objects that caught her eye.

Before dinner we were given a tour of Philip's studio. There too everything was in its place, but it was a casual order and not oppressively neat. His painting wall was empty. There were storage racks along one side, and storage spaces for paint and materials under the windows on the other. Behind his long desk he had pinned a number of recent drawings, and the painter's hodgepodge of postcard reproductions. His Piero battle scenes from the Arezzo frescoes were in plastic box frames. He hauled out a few recent paintings, but it was time for dinner and not serious looking.

We ate a simple and delicious dinner at their kitchen table. Philip cooked chicken cutlets, and we still use his recipe. We talked of food and their travels in Italy, which led to a bottle of grappa. Philip and I took this back to the studio, where Beverly and Musa joined us for a few hours until they tired.

The grappa flowed as one painting led to another. The volume of work staggered me. I saw many pictures that night that have still not been shown. Images of a gray-haired painter working at his easel with a cat-o'-nine-tails brush have stayed in my mind. His hair is stringy, like a mop head, and supple. He smokes, and Guston and I puffed away as we talked about his trials and pleasures. This painter made me think he was an animal trainer, a sort of Clyde Beatty putting images through their paces.

I wanted to see more of the "pure" drawings, and Philip lifted a stack from one of the metal storage drawers. Wordlessly we turned these over. There were a few duds in the batch, ones that, as he said, "didn't come off," but most had an elegant, muscular rightness. The tarry black lines on snowy white paper might have been precious, but the suave bulk of Guston's line and its action, the wrist and arm

75

driving it, made the forms physical. I felt I could pick up some of these images and turn them over in my hands as I might an interestingly shaped stone. The best of these drawings vibrated with the pleasure of an impulse caught, an inspiration nailed.

When we finished the grappa and smoked the last of our cigarettes it was late. Beverly and I were in the guest room off the studio, and, excited by all that I had seen and a little drunk, I lay awake, unable to sleep. I do not remember what if anything I thought, but I can still see the small painting of two barrel-chested brick houses, like the houses in my Boston neighborhood, among the small paintings covering the guest room wall. I remember that I imagined that painting on our kitchen wall.

I awoke with a hangover and after showering crossed to the kitchen for breakfast. We had come thinking we were invited for the weekend, but over coffee I got the impression that we were supposed to leave. Perhaps before lunch. This spooked me. I motioned to Beverly that I wanted to take a walk. Outside, we started to cross the road. A car came toward us. I wanted to throw myself in front of it. My hands shook. I felt about to fly apart, and began to gasp for breath.

I knew this was an anxiety attack similar to the severe one I had suffered the year before in Rochester, New York. As at that time, a piece of my mind watched while the rest of me went out of control. Beverly did her best to calm me. I said I wanted to know if we were expected to leave, but I could not ask. I complained that I was outside myself and that I felt full and empty. I wanted to cry, and to run into the woods, and to do something violent to hurt myself. I apologized for every contrary impulse.

Beverly thought it best to go inside and see if the Gustons had a tranquilizer (the ones prescribed for me after Rochester were home in Boston) and determine their plans. I was in torment, not wanting to upset them, wanting to get some relief, and uncertain if I could sit still while Beverly left me. She went inside while I fought to stifle the urges that came in spasms, and she soon came back with a pill. I took it and looked at the junk below the wall next to the potter's studio where I sat. I knew the pill would not work, and then it did. We were expected to spend only one night. Had not this been clear?

Beverly went to pack, and I, my wild thoughts subsided, went in to explain to Philip. He waved my apologies aside. He too had such attacks. We talked in the living room, and I asked a series of questions designed to get him to give me a painting or drawing. I do not think I was totally conscious of this at the time, but by that night I knew this was what I had been after. "Have you ever lent anyone a picture?" "No." Some of my flattery was just as unsubtle. I never knew what, if anything, he thought of my behavior. Soon we had lunch, and as I went to carry our bags to the car he was in his studio swabbing pink on a freshly tacked up canvas. He held a brush as we embraced and said good-bye, and was at work as we drove away.

• • •

Much later I became ashamed of my attempting to cajole a painting from Philip. I suppose I wanted a sign of affection from him, and some reward for what the anxiety attack had just put me through. At times I have guessed that I wanted Philip to be my father in art, and that, overstimulated by the night before, I was desperate for some sort of acknowledgment from him.

I recount this episode here not for what it says about Philip, but because I initially censored it. In fact, I was unwilling to write a word of it through the first four drafts of this book. My shame was that great and certainly my fear as well that the episode might either show Philip in a bad light or cast doubt on the nature of our friendship. I mean, how much a friend could I have been if I secretly wanted to be his son?

He was, I think, helpful and matter of fact in dealing with me. My anxiety could not have been as upsetting to him as it was to me. I doubt that he read into it all that I did. Why would he? At any rate the compulsion not to write about the event enlarged its significance in my mind. At the least having as a friend someone who has been a hero can be a source, as on this occasion, of bewilderment.

One Shots I

While through the seventies Guston usually stuck with an image until he exhausted it, he also produced a number of maverick paintings. So open was he that he entertained any impulse. If he imagined it, he painted it. Some of the most compelling works are one shots. When the next Guston retrospective arrives there may well be an abundance of these we have never seen before.

FLATLANDS (1970)

This hung in the Marlborough show and contains two hooded figures, but it stands apart from the Klan paintings because it is a compendium of late sixties and early seventies imagery. Bricks fly, an orange sun rises, a "pure" painting hangs from the sky, and posts, one topped with crooked nails, litter the dumplike landscape. A red Mickey Mouse–style glove/hand's fat forefinger points right. Two clocks, one numbered and one not, tick. A brick chimney smokes. Near the painting's center a pink foot is poised forward. Plaster cast or Roman ruin? A thimble-shaped lump of red has an ear, making it a head. Two legs akimbo in pools of blood might be the Klan's work. There is a squashed basketball and numerous shapes only recognizable as junk. The two nebbishlike hooded figures stare at each other in a landscape that seems home to them.

No books, no cigarettes, and no story, just a display of things Guston loved to paint. It recalls the plaster casts he heaped together at the Otis Art Institute and the painting of all the stuff in his New York studio he painted through one long day in the fifties only to scrape it off the next. *Flatlands* also looks ahead to the dumps and junk-choked ravines he drew and painted at the very end. But it is a more exuberant picture, presenting a throng, a busy street done for the hell of it, to see what these things looked like on their own together. No narrative except those supplied by things as you find them.

Here, it seems to say, is my vocabulary. You know these words as well as I do and can combine them in any way you want.

HAT (1976)

The March–April 1976 back-to-back shows at McKee that introduced the leg paintings and *Source*, Guston's portrait of his wife, Musa, included several one shots. *Shoeheads* is a permutation of the many double portraits Guston did of himself and Musa. These shoes' soles are heads because they are parted in the middle like the part in a head of hair. Behind them is the busy brushing that indicates much erasure. The heads rise from a horizon line like weird mushrooms. *Cherries* is a line of stemmed cherries solid as cannonballs. A heap of these reappears in a late acrylic as cherry bombs playing Chardin. *Hat* is by far the strangest of this group of one shots. It shows a fedora like those worn with zoot suits. Here it sits on the ground, where tracks, perhaps trolley tracks, run under it, and there are sagging wires above it. I think of this painting as taking place in the late forties. There is nothing mysterious about it but its existence. The paint, as in so many late Gustons, glistens, and the eye skates across it. Is this a holiday from the demanding leg paintings? That makes sense, but tells me nothing about why *Hat* stays in my mind. Perhaps it is the calm of this hat, blown off by the wind and settled upright in the street. It might be a borsalino Guston saw in Italy on his first trip there in the late forties, but the painting has no air of nostalgia or memory. Perhaps it sticks in my mind because it is one of those images we remember in spite of ourselves. Many late Guston images have this quality. It is a quality you cannot will into your paintings: you can only recognize it when it is there. It is a quality that comes, I suppose, when the usual distance between us and an object has been erased.

Perhaps I can illustrate this. Over thirty years ago I went by ferry from Denmark to Sweden and spent the afternoon in Göteborg. I remember nothing of that afternoon but a young mother in a green

79

suit and black hat entering a store. I stood too far from her to have any memory of her face. She is her smart green suit and fashionable black hat. This is easy to write down, but what is difficult to capture, and is the very quality Guston's *Hat* captures, is the powerful clarity of that woman as object. She means nothing to me but that clarity. Neither she nor the hat is sign or symbol, but some pure experience of shape and color broken off, in effect, from the usual way I see. This is the closest I can come to the quality of Guston's picture.

PYRAMID AND SHOE (1977)

On the wall of Guston's kitchen hung reproductions of Dürer's *Melancholia,* Piero's *Flagellation,* a postcard size de Chirico arcade scene, a classical Picasso nude, and a photograph of the Sphinx with one of the pyramids behind it. In *Pyramid and Shoe* Guston replaces the Sphinx with a double-soled work boot, a more familiar but just as enigmatic an object. The industrial faces the ancient world. An empty boot is as much a monument and has as many memorial implications as one of the pyramids. Pyramid and boot stand on red ground against a much painted gray sky into which the blue that follows a storm spreads. There is a solid dignity and grounded thereness to both objects. I think of Blake's proverb "Where man is not nature is barren." Pyramid and work boot are what man leaves in nature to remind himself he has been there and can endure. Both attest to the enormous effort of this undertaking. What originally justified such effort is usually forgotten, and we struggle to find a reason to explain why such things exist. Guston cares nothing for reasons. That the imagination must have it so is enough for him.

The last night I saw Guston alive, just as we let him out at his hotel, he turned to say that he hoped to live as long as Titian and to take a boat down the Nile and visit all that "marvelous, massive sculpture."

David McKee Gallery

An artist and his dealer are like a married couple except they never have a happy marriage — this is how Guston described the relationship between artist and dealer to me. When he pulled out of Marlborough he went unrepresented in New York until 1974. David McKee, who had worked at Marlborough, then became his dealer, and while their marriage had its strains it endured, and McKee represents Guston to this day.

McKee's first gallery, the space he maintained through the seventies, was in the Hotel Barbizon across Lexington Avenue on Sixty-third Street and off the beaten track. It was a small, awkwardly divided space on the mezzanine near a dress shop. Columns stood in the way, and the floor was covered in linoleum. Not exactly Siberia but far enough out of it to feel like exile, for Guston an honorable state.

Although Guston dreamt of buying a derelict brick mill or factory upstate near his Woodstock home and turning it into a museum for his work ("I could bus my friends up"), at McKee's he could show in New York and still feel aloof from the art world.

Between November 1974 and Guston's death, McKee hung six shows, including a museum-scale retrospective of drawings. In total McKee exhibited by my count sixty-two drawings and forty-six paintings—a pittance compared with what Guston produced during those years. In March and April 1976 McKee showed fourteen paintings completed in 1975. At the show Guston told Jerry Tallmer of the *New York Post* that he had painted forty-five "large paintings" that year. He certainly painted several hundred large paintings in the seventies and as many smaller ones. His late drawings must number in the thousands.

Although Guston's prices were not high for the time, few of his works sold, and this helped bring about his return to teaching. Perhaps because Guston's work so occupied him, he taught, according to several ex-students, with passion, lucidity, and force. Young painters often felt their effort valued regardless of how severely Guston criticized individual paintings. He had a way of seeing through the art in someone's work to what was original. This often meant that he focused on the work his students felt was painted out of some impulse they themselves could not identify. Since Guston lived and breathed painting with such intensity he must have scared off as many students as he inspired. Either way it is unlikely that many who encountered Guston as a teacher came away shortchanged. If he did not give his students a leg up he must have given them a wall to go around.

The two times I visited his Woodstock studio I was amazed by the rows of finished canvases leaning against one another and filed away in storage racks. Both of us huffed and puffed and had to be very careful as we swung paintings around so as not to bash them. One painting I saw on my summer visit has stayed with me because it caught something of Guston's anxiety about the art, teaching, and painting worlds in which he sometimes uneasily lived.

On a reddish pink ground stands a small table, an end table, holding a black rotary telephone and a bacon and egg sandwich. Guston liked going to a local greasy spoon for such sandwiches, a look through the papers, and the conversation of the regulars. About the phone he was ambivalent. Loathing its interruptions but unable to live without it, he had the switch installed enabling him to shut it off to incoming calls. He liked to go days with a dead line, and liked to brag about this as an example of how far he would go to hide out from the world.

In this painting Guston sanded down the phone and the sandwich so they were ghosts of themselves. Yet the phone retains its solid heft and the strips of bacon dangle, mouthwateringly, fresh off the grill, chewy and crisp. Loving to talk and eat as he did, Guston may have come back from the diner to paint both his pleasures and the discipline he enforced on himself. He could consume the sandwich, enjoying his forays into the world where it was made, but he could be consumed by the phone and the requests and offers that came over it.

Still, he was not quite the recluse he liked to picture himself as. One night he complained to me about a dinner BU had planned to honor him with to be held at McKee's. He had agreed, and now he did not want to go. He knew BU wanted to take advantage of his name and fill the gallery with prospective donors. This clearly flattered him, and it seemed to annoy him that he was flattered. He went into a song and dance. At times, I think, he wanted what the phone brought, but he did not want to be seen as wanting it. His appetite for the world he needed to reject perplexed him. I remember how pleased he was that Dick Cavett asked him to be interviewed on his talk show and how doubly pleased that he had said no.

During that same 1977 visit to Guston's studio I saw several of the paintings of sleepers in bed, a run he was deep into at the time. Either these were self-portraits or he was in bed with Musa. He showed me more than a dozen of these images on a sunny midsummer afternoon. He was dressed for painting, paint-spattered shirttails out, and he told me he often slept in the shirt, waking to pull on his pants and walk, sockless, right to the studio, where he painted himself in the bed he had just left. Only one of these pictures, *Red Blanket,* appeared in the 1980 retrospective, and none ever made its way into a McKee show.

When I last saw Guston in late March of 1980, we met in his room at the Ritz, the other end of Newbury Street from the Hotel Eliot, where BU usually put him up. He had recovered from his first heart attack and regained weight, but he was clearly older and haggard around the eyes. Nerves over his upcoming retrospective gave him license to smoke. We talked of his time in the hospital, and he described his hallucination that the hospital payroll was being robbed by a gang of thieves that he alone was on to. He raised hell trying to get the nurses' attention but could not convince them to help him foil the plot. The "gang" turned out to be security guards visiting the nurses' station for coffee. It was as if an episode his illness prevented him from painting had to be acted out.

And he spoke of his retrospective opening in June in San Francisco. I had never heard him speak with such anticipation about a show. He was already enjoying it as he never seemed to have enjoyed his McKee shows. Those, I think, not only sparked all his anxieties about his place in the art world but felt shapeless to him, unsatisfying and like pieces broken off the main of his work. The retrospective's emphasis on the late work, with over half the paintings painted after 1968, made it a vindication. His tone said, This will show them. Seen in mass, the work, he believed, would sweep aside the now clearly uninformed judgments of his critics. In the future, he mused, he wanted an even larger show of only late work but not just — he chuckled — "my masterpieces." He wanted, he explained, people to see the work in context, "the world" of the work, and to present a sense of how images had insisted themselves on him, been pursued, abandoned, stuck with, and fixed so paint held them.

• • •

One day in the late seventies, it was at the McKee Gallery that Guston stood before *Attar* which had a price tag of $90,000. Morton Feldman and his wife, in the midst of their divorce, had the painting up for sale. Guston came to Boston the next day still flabbergasted at the price. "Ninety thousand," he repeated several times, as if he had to drum into his head the reality of such an astronomical figure. It clearly stunned him. This was the one time in our friendship that Guston spoke of money in relation to his art, and the only time I knew him to be speechless.

Surrealism, etc.

*Anyway, all art is a kind of hallucination, but
hallucination with work. Or dreaming with your
eyes open.*

— PHILIP GUSTON

The influence of surrealism is apparent on the early work of de
Kooning, Rothko, and Pollock, but on Guston it left little trace.
In the forties he drew on Uccello and Max Beckmann. If de Chirico,
an enthusiasm since his late teens, imparted a sense of space as mood
and a melancholy urban poetry, Guston's images of children at play-
war could have come from kids in his neighborhood. Indeed, his
daughter is a central figure in *If This Be Not I.*

By the seventies, when surrealism had become a synonym for weird
and stood for any strange coincidence or event out of the ordinary,
Guston embraced the theory of the movement while dismissing its
products. The surrealist emphasis on the unconscious appealed to
him, but he found the paintings and the objects too often formulaic.
Surrealist images struck him as examples tailored to support the
theory. They did not seem to come from the place where the theory
said they should. Perhaps they seemed too cerebral to be unconscious.

Since his own work came with increasing force from somewhere
within him the word *imagination* seemed inadequate to describe, the
unconscious appeared its likely source. Why shoes? Why spaghetti
clumps of legs, paws brandishing shields, and heads swept away in
a flood? And what was the connection between them? While his
desire to see and to make could not be any more conscious, the late
work presents much that could not come direct from the visible world.
We see shoes every day, but not a tangle of naked legs or warriors
with paws.

A remarkable aspect of these images is how they refuse the mystery associated with surrealist art. They do not exist in a dreamworld. The unconscious is not in a Guston painting as it is in a Magritte or an Ernst. The viewer looking at a burning tuba or bird's head on a man's body thinks "unconscious." Guston's images leave behind the place from which they came. The legs, for example, state themselves straightforwardly. They take us for granted, are not coy, and never let us think we are eavesdropping. Guston's images are so forthright, so squarely in the light of day that we feel we ought to know them and that they must be passages from a familiar narrative. Nothing this clear ought to puzzle us so. It is their clarity that spooks us.

The 1977 painting *Legend* shows Guston's trust in the unconscious. On the extreme right the painter sleeps. A book lies open on his bed. He must have fallen asleep in midsentence. Perhaps the other images are from the book. They fill the rest of the canvas, creating a welter, a warehouse, of images. A horse's rear end — remembered from Caravaggio? — moseys off the dream stage. We see its out-thrust tail and upraised hoof. There is a bottle, cigarette butts, a shoe sole, two spilling cans, a brick, and a triangular board with protruding nails — Guston's usual junk. A disembodied hand swings a nightstick, another fisted hand plunges down, and a hairy paw lifts a shield. The images are helter-skelter. They neither narrate a story nor glow of the "strange." The painting could serve as a sign over a shop selling dreamware.

Legend erases the line between conscious and unconscious. The images are both those released in sleep and those carried from waking into sleep and, as we look at the painting, from sleep into our awake eye. Guston dreams and he dreams up. It is the program of surrealism with its art, without any self-conscious adherence to doctrine. Because surrealism sought to legitimize the unconscious as the true source of art there is an element of argument in its art. Guston had no such need to legitimize nor to argue. He did not have to exalt or advertise his unconscious, but could take it for granted.

The Studio (1969)

Painting, Smoking, Eating (1973)

Monument (1976)

Source (1976)

Pyramid and Shoe (1977)

Painter's Forms (1972)

Painter's Table, Painter's Forms, I and II

On the table in *Painter's Table* are set out books, shoe soles, railroad spikes, a paint-daubed palette, an ashtray full of butts, two old-fashioned hand irons of the kind you place on a stove to heat up, and a finished canvas of a single wide-open eye. The painter still works, for a smoking cigarette is perched on the table's edge. Through a window we see the night outside. A single bulb hangs over the table. We know these things. Nothing is out of the ordinary except the finished canvas, and even that is familiar. Guston's late work abounds in eyes, or the single eye, bug eye, sometimes bleary with fatigue, the painter's eye that never shuts.

Yet this eye may be a note, a reminder to paint a larger version. Or it is the eye that keeps watch on the painter; the eye under whose gaze paintings are painted, the all-seeing, all-knowing eye to which the painter submits and by whose grace he works. A household god. The painter is on good terms with it for now, but as he works, it will be there to look back at him.

A world of eyes, but for someone of Guston's orality there are few mouths in his work. *Painter's Forms* (1972) and *Painter's Forms II* (1978) are the exceptions. In its simplicity, *Painter's Forms* is like *Legend*. Eyes closed, the openmouthed head has coughed up several common Guston forms. Because of its resemblance to the figure that mocks Christ in Fra Angelico's San Marco monk's cell fresco, the head may be cursing, cursing the painter by giving him these homely forms—a shoe to kick with, a bottle to drink from, and a length of scrap wood. They have been expelled in no clear order and seem to be parts of speech upon which the painter must impress his syntax.

As these forms popped out, violently as if bottled up for some time, there is also something explosive about *Painter's Forms II*. Legs and body parts spill out of the open mouth. No telling how long this disgorgement will last nor how much there is inside to come out. The painter cannot help himself as he vomits forth this mess of entrails that seem to be coming from deep inside, that might even be his guts, liver, and lights. Has the painter no control? Is he speaking these forms or are they speaking him?

Sudden, barking expulsion has given way to a slow, relentless flow. In neither case does the painter, the mouth, seem to have a choice. He has gorged himself on images as we all have, and now he must work with what comes not down from above like a lightning bolt of inspiration but up from below. Who knows what has sat down there until the forms appear? The painter's art pours forth. He has no choice but to let it come, and no matter if it disgusts him to work with it faithfully under the alert eye in his studio.

"Locates, Suggests, Discovers"

What is believed to be boldness is only awkwardness. So liberty is really the impossibility of following the path which everyone takes and following the one your talents make you take.

— Henri Matisse

"Usually, I draw in relation to my paintings," and so Guston did in the fifties, when he made this statement. This relationship changed in the late sixties. Guston entered the tangible world of his late works through drawing. Painting, as he said, "settled the issues" his drawings had explored in those years, but drawing continued to have a life of its own.

Not that Guston stopped working up paintings from drawings. Several of these studies found their way into the McKee drawing show. But now he did a number of large drawing projects, including his biography of Richard Nixon and the collaboration with Clark Coolidge, and made a great many drawings for their own sake.

These finished late drawings communicate the pleasure Guston must have enjoyed in doing them. It is a pleasure taken in the smallest mark and repeated detail. The viewer feels how much Guston loved drawing the hanging lightbulb's snaky cord, spider's webs, stitching in the Klan hoods, whiskers, eyelets in shoes and nail heads in shoe heels and soles, words in books, book pages, smoke, creased brows and puffed out cheeks, rough-hewn ladders, the wood grain in waste board, scrolls, tenpenny nails and the wide heads of spikes, bristling paws, paintbrushes thick enough to lather on shaving cream, clock hands pointed like arrowheads, his wife's parted hair, the sun shaped like a wheel . . . to list them is to delight in finding words to mimic their intensely physical presence and graspable immediacy.

"I wanted to be complete again," Guston said, "as I was when I was a kid . . ." The late drawings combine this desire and its fulfillment. The best are as effortless as an athlete's flawless play, fifty years of practice become innate grace. They have the child's total concentration that we lose, remember ardently, and must struggle to regain. Talent is never enough. It takes years of doing to earn the confidence Guston displays here and to draw so that the mark is the thought.

So thin is the acrylic on Guston's very last works that it is more a wash coloring drawings than painting. Magdalena Dabrowski found room for these in her Museum of Modern Art drawing retrospective. They tempt one to see and argue drawing as the soul of Guston's late work. Those who emphasize the cartoon quality of his images seem stuck on this proposition. But, for me at least, the image does not dominate Guston's brush. There is a unity, and I think Guston realized an old dream and made drawing and painting one. His brush may have, must have, gained confidence from his pen, but once it did he never looked back. The eye runs like a hand over this lavish paint as the mind apprehends the image's rough vitality.

So rich is the give-and-take between Guston's drawing and painting that another way to consider the relationship suggests itself. John Berger wrote that "painting interrogates the visible." If this is true I can hear Guston's licks of paint asking the questions that his drawing has formed.

One Shots II

BOX AND SHADOW (1978)

Before her death in April 1992, Musa Guston gave over ninety Gustons, most of them late works, to museums in the United States and abroad. *Box and Shadow* is one of four bequests to New York's Museum of Modern Art. There are raucous Gustons — the Klansmen and the legs — and silent ones. He could cram a painting with incident —*The Street* is an example — or put in no more than enough, as in *Hat. Box and Shadow* is one of the latter. The background looks like Guston just wanted to push paint around that day and get a gorgeous surface. Above a red wall there is an ivory-pink sky as luminous and appetizing as fresh cake frosting. It is hard to keep from swiping a finger full. The foreground mixes this sky with red from the wall, and here the box sits in a beautiful land. It has been hammered together from boards and could be a shipping crate. It casts a greasy black shadow. On the box's top a spider shaped like an M walks. Sky, wall, box, shadow, and spider are as instantly alive as this second's unexpected thought. Guston liked to quote Leonardo's maxim "Painting is a thing of the mind." If it is then that mind must feel the things pictured as mind does in looking at *Box and Shadow,* and the painting must shine forth matter's sensuous reality.

TRACK (1978)

Black above. Black below. A gray band runs through the black like a tunnel through coal. A black line, the track, divides the gray like the white line divides a highway. A third of the way in from the left a red foot, sore or ancient or both, kicks a white ball the size of a softball. Not kicks but taps the ball carefully to keep it on track. The ball's progress appears slow, a matter of inches. Perhaps it is a progress too small to measure because it is infinitesimal to the eye. When we return tomorrow or next week we may swear the ball has not moved. In a month or a year we will forget where it was when we last saw it and be unable to gauge how far it has come.

Guston liked to say that he moved not by leaps but slowly, that he was not a kangaroo but an inchworm. It could be his naked foot in *Track* keeping the ball in play. He labored to take risks, which is another of his paradoxes. Slowly, slowly he moved through trial and error until the outcome felt intuited. Those of us who had to wait for new paintings to appear in galleries or museums were likely to think each new batch of Gustons a series of leaps. He knew better.

PULL (1979)

The lightbulb in *Pull* is nearly drowned by jelly-thick blackness. This is night the traveler must part with his hands, and push his way through. There is a sliver of sky above and green earth below. The bulb's bead chain is chunky like gold nuggets strung together. You might, waving both hands in the blackness, get a good grip on it. But if you pulled you might erase the sky and leave all black, or light up everything. I take the ominous approach. Leave the chain alone! The murk of the black and the earthen green turf and the sky belong as is; they are forever. It is the bulb and chain that do not belong. We live out and we live under their short light, a light that every day is more obscured by natural forces. Let it shine as long as it will and ask nothing more from it.

Outside Reliance, South Dakota, I once saw a terrible black storm come over the green prairie. It began to pound rain, and the black seemed rippling muscle or meat. I pulled over and watched the black sky draw green from the grass as it came toward me. It began to hail as this monster of nature got over the car. A moment later and the black-green muscle had rolled over me. The sun came out blinding and hot as I drove toward it, crunching the remnants of hail. I see this storm when I look at *Pull*.

Marriage

It was a snowy February afternoon when Jon Imber, then Guston's student, dropped Philip off at my house. He had come from a slide talk at the University of Minnesota and was greatly agitated. Not about art but about his wife, Musa. She had suffered a stroke. "It's always been art, art, art, but now it has to be life, life, life. I'll give up painting. I'll do anything if she'll get better."

Musa did regain her health, surviving her husband by a dozen years, and living to see Guston's late work filled with images of her famous in the world. She spent most of her last years in their Woodstock home beside his studio. She once told Beverly that she and Philip liked to sleep in the guest bedroom off the studio every few months so as to smell the oil paint and remember their lofts and apartments in New York.

At her memorial service Ross Feld recalled how much those who knew her wanted her good opinion. Not because she was forbidding or stern, for she was surpassingly mild, but because she embodied, in her quiet way, moral authority. She seemed to know instinctively right from wrong and sense from nonsense. "Ohh, nooo, Philip," said in a shy, scolding tone reeled in her husband when he proposed, for instance, that he fill his pictures with the names of poet and painter heroes — Piero, T. S. Eliot, and Masaccio written like sky-writing. She made you feel that nothing but your best was worthy of you. She did this by force of character. She did nothing for effect, and had not a false move in her small, delicate body.

In most of the obvious ways Philip and Musa were opposites. He was voluble, a world-class talker, and she was soft-spoken, quiet to the point of self-erasure. He talked endlessly of art and his work. If you did not know she wrote poetry, you would not learn it from her. He was six feet tall and burly. She was perhaps five two, beautifully wrinkled with blond-gray hair and as feminine in gesture as he was masculine. The commonplace that old married couples grow to look alike could not have been proven by Philip and Musa.

Their marriage split (it was Philip's doing) in the midsixties, but it did not break apart. The adoring image of Musa and the unity of man and woman throughout the late work represent, to some degree, the feeling Guston had for she who had been steadfast, wronged but true, through difficult and wayward years. A common late image is Musa's head joined to Philip's by a spider's web.

Early one morning Musa had pointed out a large, impressively detailed web in the grass off their back deck. Fascinated, Guston studied it, and brought the web into his work. As he rarely found images in nature, the spider and web must have had some special resonance for him. They might be seen as life going about its business, unmindful of human affairs. We are caught in such webs as Philip and Musa were caught in the web of years, joined and held there by the spinning spider, who cares not at all that he joins them. For our part we can hardly feel the spider's fine threads.

Guston's webs remind us of how much is not in our control and of how much takes place outside our awareness. Spiders ensnare us as the years spin on. As an emblem of marriage the web wittily places the unity of husband and wife outside their hands. They look up and they are closer than they ever thought they were, bound by the spider's patient art. Age too is their bond as the spider works best where the sharp movements of youth do not disturb him.

But this is an image of much sadness as well, for the spider suggests how decrepit the heads have become. As spiders do their work in dark and dank places, their webs are associated with the forgotten, the dead and entombed. Prized unity comes when we can no longer resist it. The paradox is that the spider unites us because we do not have the energy to pull ourselves apart. Inertia has a somewhat positive outcome.

In painting after painting, Musa's golden head rises like a horseshoe sun, image of luck and life, from the sea or blue horizon line. She is the sun in Guston's most memorable image of her, *Source*. Against a terra-cotta background she rises, a green halo framing her head, over blue water. The colors are elemental, ancient. This Musa is nature and art. Nothing could be simpler than her presence. The painter's adoration for her is unabashed. Her eyes lift heavenward, and yet (this is the genius of the painting) they cast their light in steps across the water to those who stand before, and to the painter. Musa is goddess and muse.

Source could have been found on a cave or tomb wall. Or on a billboard advertising the first morning of the world. It appeared in public for the first time at the entrance to Guston's 1976 March–April back-to-back shows at McKee. You were invited to imagine that all that followed emerged from service to this sun goddess. But what strange offerings! Shod, naked legs stomping on scatter rugs! Legs kept in line by a disembodied hand wielding a nightstick! And there was *Pit* into which the legs, hooves up, had plunged beside a head whose eye stared downward. Hell flames blazed up like bookends bracketing a finished seascape, which looked like an image off the television screen. Out of the sublime *Source* came such dread and images of a sensibility overwhelmed.

As I look back, the juxtaposition suggests a connection I missed at the time. To the painter, under her gaze, the source grants permission to paint anything he imagines. Her gaze is unconditional. It demands only that his art respect no condition that will restrict it. We know of Guston's rushing Musa into his studio to see what he had painted, what he had "done," as if he feared himself an accomplice to some crime. We know that he was not just after admiration. We know of her lifelong devotion to his work and of her (the eyes of

Source are on the heavens!) ability to discriminate and to see what the painter made independent of the painter. *Source* celebrates this serenity that Guston so needed as a balance to his high-strung, jittery brilliance.

So entwined was Musa with Guston's art that one of his first responses to her stroke was to leave David McKee's gallery. McKee was not the problem. "Nothing occurred other than my decision," Guston wrote me while waiting for Musa's return from the hospital, "to be out of the art 'scene' altogether. Shows in San Francisco and Los Angeles were canceled. My strongest desire is to make the 'career' part of being a painter altogether irrelevant, hopefully putting all energy into the work itself — whether anyone sees it or not." Fear, panic, and guilt are implicit here, and so is the desire to bring his art, the part of his life he could control, home. When Musa's condition improved Guston returned his work to McKee and reentered the art world with images of the spider spinning its web.

Smoke

The hero of *Smoke* paints, dressed like a matinee idol with ascot smooth at his throat and wavy hair slicked back. You can see its sheen and smell the pomade with which he has dressed it. His single eye is fiery red. He has been up all night and may have just come in from a nightspot. There is a blue morning sky in the background, but lightbulbs festoon the space overhead. This painter needs all the light he can get.

Like other Guston heads of 1978 and after, this one belongs to a veteran. His rough, stubbled cheeks are scored and patched. His large ear is misshapen and raw. He is dressed like a third-rate actor's idea of an actor. Painting is his performance, his night on the town. He has dressed for it, bringing his illusion of himself to the illusion he is creating.

95

Columbus Square Journal...

WILLIAM CORBETT

He is balanced between two worlds. Half of him rests on the crude wooden floor of a painter's loft, and the other half, the painting half, floats on water. A brick wall, loaded brushes piled before it and a drawn green shade atop it, stands behind the painter. He paints with two brushes at once. His concentration is demonic. He is red enough to explode. He smokes one cigarette and holds another, from which reddish gray, meaty smoke rises. He is a dapper engine of art.

No other Guston image of the artist at work is as theatrical. If art is hallucination, then this is the hallucinator, and he knows it, and furthermore he knows how to get into character. In *The Studio* the curtain lifts to expose the Klansman-painter, but he does not know we are watching. The painter in *Smoke* treads the boards with the energy of George Jessel or Milton Berle. He is making a night of it and wants his audience to admire his every move.

His stage is outdoors and indoors. Solid floorboards stop at water, or a lake of wet, scraped-off paint. Carnival lightbulbs hang from the sky. A brick wall . . . it is impossible to tell where the studio is, and the painter is dressed to go out but . . . well, what can be said is that the painter is working double-time. So frenzied is he that he may not know where he is nor care. James Thurber said he could write upside down in a boiler room, and this painter could work alongside him. He has done this a million times and has the scars to prove it. The old warhorse and ham has gotten up onstage again. He is up for the act that demands he play all the roles before shuffling off the stage. "When you are working," Guston liked to quote his friend John Cage, "everybody is in your studio — the past, your friends, the art world, and above all your own ideas — all are there. But as you continue painting, they start leaving, one by one, and you are left completely alone. Then, if you are lucky, even you leave." The painter in *Smoke* is dressed to get lucky.

In the film of H. Rider Haggard's *She,* Guston had a bit part as a high priest. Some critics have deemed this prophetic and cast Guston as a tormented soul who laid down God's law and made pronouncements as if he alone had a direct line to what painting really is. The embattled Guston might have had little sense of humor about his work, but the work has a keen sense of humor. Guston's doubt, to paraphrase Henry James, was his passion.

"I Am the Subject"

Do not let me hear
Of the wisdom of old men, but rather of their folly

— T. S. ELIOT, "EAST COKER"

The artist in his studio, a subject untouched by Guston in nearly forty years of painting, is omnipresent in his late work. So prevalent is it that some critics and art historians have come to see it in Guston all along and have ferreted out a painter standing at his easel in several abstract paintings. The urge to show that Guston's art was really all of a piece, that through the changes he remained the same is, for some, that irresistible.

Although Guston goes at the subject in a number of ways, several key props appear in *The Studio,* the first of the pictures to pick up this theme. The artist, though day can be seen through the window, works under a single, naked lightbulb. We have seen this lightbulb in countless movies. It signifies poverty, cheap hotel rooms, anonymous transient spaces, and the back rooms and cellars where police conduct interrogations. It is also the bulb that illuminates solitary confinement. For Guston it had childhood associations as he remembered hiding in a closet drawing under such a bulb.

A clock hangs from the studio wall, its visible hand an arrow. A similar clock, but numbered, appears in *Studio Landscape.* Yes, the painter is obsessed by time. He is under the gun, trying to make every moment count. Guston certainly heard the clock ticking and minded the passing hours, but he was as mindful of the history of painting. He kept one eye on the clock of painting, "that," he once said, "sees each end of the street as the edge of the world."

There are paintbrushes stuck in paint cans, the unglamorous tools of the painter's trade. In other pictures brushes sit in disarray, lying where they were dropped, on a painter's table. They are sometimes heaped together, and in the foreground of *Moon* they are arched like thick worms with bright-colored heads crawling. To all these brushes Guston gives that peculiar, affecting physical presence common to all the objects he painted. You lift his books in your mind; you imagine your foot fitting into one of his brogans, and you reach to pick up these brushes in your hand.

The painting Klansman in *The Studio*, one of the "little bastards" as Guston called these hooded figures, smokes as he works. Guston's painter is invariably a chain smoker, and cigarettes burn in these paintings the way they do in thirties and forties movies. When the painter is through he leaves an ashtray overflowing butts. These measure the hours and intensity of his work, and they are his signature.

Lightbulbs, clock, paintbrushes, cigarettes. Add to these stretchers, a painter's table, a painting being worked on, and the painter at work. These are the lineaments of Guston's studio pictures. He never works from a model or arrangement of objects. Images come from his imagination to be discovered and combined on canvas.

As the Klan paintings end, the painter is revealed. He has a large, bulbous head and is a grizzled middle-aged man. His face is swollen with effort, and his single bloodshot eye is agog, its eyeball huge, black, and pupilless like Picasso's. This is the head of a painter crammed to exploding with images and the frustrations of making them come out right. He has been up all night and has hours still to go. We see only his head and his brush-holding, cigarette-holding hand. Head and hand. Inspiration and execution. Nothing in between to disturb the circuit. In several paintings the painter works with such vehemence his brush is a whip, and painting has the whip hand.

This is a painter who cannot leave his work in the studio. Asleep in bed beside his wife, he wears shoes and his wristwatch and clutches brushes. If a dream hits him he is prepared. On the covers of *Couple in Bed* sits a wooden triangle. It has no reason to be there. Could it suggest the triangle of painter, wife, and painting?

The painter is driven, enthralled to his art. He cannot keep from painting and must face every subject that occurs to him. In *Moon* the painter's white hair stands on end like the hair of someone frightened in a science-fiction movie. He works on one canvas and a second stands nearby. Thick-handled brushes squirm in the foreground. They are alive. Behind the painter, bugs crawl over a ravine. He has turned away from the horror of their maggoty work to paint it, scared stiff by what he has seen and will soon see again on his canvas.

The driven painter lets us see that after you have spent your life searching out inspiration, that deepest source within you, and you find that source, the contact is adhesive and you cannot turn it on and off at will. These paintings are a visual counterpart to Samuel Beckett's agonized resolution "I can't go on, I'll go on." And yet this is the position Guston longed to be in. He reveals his secret world as he discovers and meditates upon the nature of that world. A strange, tense, yet joyous world filled, paradoxically, with the common objects that Guston comes to believe "nourished" all art. A world desired as much for its miseries as for its attendant joys — the only world for this painter.

The only world even as it slips away from him. Following his second heart attack, when he was confined to painting small acrylics, Guston's brushes, books, and shoes slide down hillsides. He paints the dump where his images, slipping from him, lie in wreckage. But these paintings also signal that his source is not yet dried up. He cannot help but follow through to the end, to see and paint his own culture sliding away from him, a culture that will not relax its grip on him.

Behind his studio door he works on as if back in the closet of his youth. His images, rolled into a ball, are at the door, knocking. He paints away, ignoring the welter of images we come to see that he will never have time to invite in, and he shows us this standoff, fascinated, as ever, by what it means to have an art. He must be at work on the very last tightly massed constructions, his images collapsed and packed for travel, or on the ladders climbing into the heavens, ladders that prepare him for the ascent as he prepares to ascend. This painter looks with such unflinching candor at his end that his pictures become as energetic as any he ever painted.

Guston's attention to the painter at work is only one of the themes in which he becomes his subject. Even he could not work round the clock through weeks and months, and when he was not working he sometimes sank into melancholy. Depression, perhaps a legacy from his father, periodically brought Guston low. When we were trading stories about our common anxiety, he told me he sometimes just broke down without warning. He recalled a spasm of uncontrollable weeping on a flight to Detroit for a show. He had, I think, convinced himself that these episodes were inexplicable, another mysterious and not to be investigated aspect of who he was. He dosed himself with drink to tame these black moods, to relax from work, and to calm the jets of his fevered imagination.

The bottle is one of the Klansmen's bad habits, and it was one of Guston's too. *Head and Bottle* is a self-portrait. The painter's open book and wet brush lie unused; he only has eyes for the green whiskey bottle. His is not the bloodshot working painter's eye but a clear, unclouded one. It is his head that is red, sore with hangover and hurt. The staring head wobbles on its whiskered chin. Mind, a bout of melancholy and drink, has overwhelmed all that matters.

It is in Michael Blackwood's superb film of Guston, *A Life Lived,* that Guston declares, as if admitting the truth, "I am the subject." I imagine him amplifying this: "Why shoes, books, ladders, garbage cans? . . . Because they are in me, and feel like they have been there for a long time. They are the touchable world I imagine and hope to bring to life, and they are the vocabulary of that world. These objects are not personal in the sense that they have any extraordinary associations for me. We spend a great deal of our lives in shoes. Books are everywhere. I am not keeping private meanings from you. These objects have a wealth of associations, and this seems to bewilder some who look at my paintings. These images come from the common storehouse. What they are in any particular painting is what they express, but nevertheless they are mine, are the forms my imagination has found release through, and they imprint my stories with this human's imagination, the tone of his voice."

For all this, we might read the very late Gustons totally independent of him. Their slag heaps could be both a memory of Eliot's wasteland and a prophecy of the ecological hell we are determined to bring upon ourselves. We could read them as admonitions that what we unearth in the attempt to show ourselves to ourselves is not fixed matter but in perpetual drift. We see, the paintings suggest, our deepest selves only as they slip from us. Junk is what we carry within us, and what we leave behind in heaps. Many late Gustons present this version of the apocalypse with a disinterested ferocity.

It is the ferocity of a painter ravenous for his work. The images have been grabbed and yanked roughly before us so great is his hunger and so quick his reach. Those who first see these images must be impressed by their brute innocence and crude forthrightness. This painter could not wait to see, and the strength of his desire is explicit. He cares little for our approval. He wants more our fascinated attention. We might be horrified, as some of these pictures convince us the painter was when he painted them. Horrified and fascinated as much by what we are seeing as by how we cannot turn away from that which we fear. Evil is fascinating to the eye and so is pain.

Guston might have completed "I am the subject" with "and paint is the verb." De Kooning proclaimed that oil paint was invented so Rubens could paint flesh. It was reinvented by Guston so he could deliver the light whose glow animates these paintings. He knew that what he called the "information" of his paintings could be quickly taken in, but that the paint slowed the mind down and let it grasp the light and feel the specific gravity of the images. This is the light that holds up, and having solidified matter into illumination, holds us. Paint may only be, as Guston liked to remind us, "colored earth," but it is just this property that the master painter transforms into light that supports us as it extends our vision. In Guston's light we look longer and deeper, and we drink in his world, thereby intensifying our own.

102

We need the steadying presence of Guston's light because Guston had to shock us to get us into his world. These paintings shock, in fact, because they refuse to accept what we think we know about painting. The eye schooled by thirty years of art world trends, eager to love and give approval, to "appreciate," slides right off a Guston. Just as Guston gave up something, so we must give up the confidence of our assumptions if we want to enter his world. For him, "getting involved in painting means to divest myself continuously of what I already know." These paintings hold the eye that longs to see as if seeing painting for the first time.

Whatever the quality for which there are words but no word, the quality that compels us to look and adhere to a painting, this mysterious pull is everywhere in late Gustons. I want to stare at these grizzled heads and go slowly over their every feature and memorize them so I can carry them away because something is in store for them and for me. As they grip me I grip them and mind is harmonized with matter, and I take the outside in.

East Coker: T.S.E.

As we grow older
The world becomes stranger, the pattern more complicated
Of dead and living.

— T. S. ELIOT

Guston did not turn away from old age and impending death. He persisted in his folly, in the explorations Eliot thought old men ought to make. In a late acrylic, a dump of signature images runs downhill to a tombstone inscribed "1980 P.G." Images he loved beat on his studio door. He painted on, making believe he did not hear them and knowing he no longer had the time to meet their demands even as he could not resist catching them in the act. There is pathos and humor in these paintings. What is the painter to do so besieged by images he has called to life? He can avoid them like laying low from Halloween trick-or-treaters for whom he has no candy and make believe no one is at home. And all the while seize on another, unexpected image like *East Coker: T.S.E.*, to paint. Perhaps it is aging that brings such images with feral intensity.

Guston painted it in 1979 in response to his first heart attack. The background is a nondescript gray quickly brushed on, an anonymous color for a space as anonymous as a hospital room or morgue. Eliot, in bed, stares up at the ceiling, his face set in a terrible rictus, a death grimace. The ear we can see is overlarge, a Buddha's ear for this wise poet. The neck is scrawny, and the gray chin stubbled in red resembles a turkey's knobby wattle. Deep lines like red fissures waste Eliot's haggard face. The strain of death, either holding it off or hoping for it to come, has worked every facial muscle into a grin.

Perhaps Eliot grins into the void, staring death down, sardonic and challenging. Maybe what is in store for us isn't so terrible after all, and the last laugh is ours as it appears to be Eliot's. Or death has twisted Eliot's features into a self-mocking grin, and the last laugh is literally on him. He has turned into a caricature of pain and fear. The image plants the thought that we can have the grin we want, but in either case death is its agent. T.S.E.'s ambiguous expression mocks our sentimental hope that death will compose our features in calm, welcoming repose. And it bitterly mocks our other hope that the final disclosure will answer our questions. As the screws of death tighten on this Eliot pain is what we see.

After Guston's death, his widow, Musa, hung this picture in her home. Some visitors were spooked enough to question her about it. They may have thought that only a dangerous morbidity could cause her to want to look at Eliot's grimace every day. Whatever she thought she must have thought others would not turn away, for on her death she gave the painting to the Museum of Modern Art.

Head

Celebrate man's craft
and the word spoken in shapeless night, the
sharp tool pairing away
waste and the forms
cut out of mystery!

— BASIL BUNTING, "ODE 15"

The eyeball kisses the brow. It looks up the long incline on which the head that holds it has come to rest. The head is mouthless, gunmetal blue, prickly with thick stubble, and patched with several bandages that look like they have been welded on. The eye can open no wider; it is a large V in the skull. There is an ear shaped like a briefcase handle. No telling what this battered head has been through. It seems to have a specific weight, the weight of a large cannonball or boulder. A man might not be able to lift it, but he could put his shoulder to it and push it along. Has it rolled down to this spot or stopped here as it rolled itself up the hill? The head shows no sign that it will soon move or be moved.

The hill is barren, grassless, but the ground is strewn with rocks, empty tin cans, a brick, an apple — rubble. Perhaps this hill ends in a junk-choked ditch. It is a familiar wasteland. Eliot, as we have seen, was much on Guston's mind, but if it is Eliot's sterile industrial desert, it is also where Beckett's tramps meet and the steppe on which Michelangelo stages *The Crucifixion of Saint Peter*.

If the ground is familiar so is the head. He is brother to all Guston's wide-eyed painters who are too keyed up to sleep in their beds and whose smoking, staring, unshaven heads have brows creased like knuckles. Their bulging eyes must witness as if it is their calling. Even recumbent these painters are never at rest. The perpetually open, fixed eye is their primary organ.

105

This last head might be under pressure from what the eye has brought inside. The welded patches must cover cracks or fissures opened by this pressure. The chin and brow have been cut by rocks and shards as the head moved over the waste ground. However the head has come to be its own Sisyphus, it has been knocked about inside and out on its way.

Guston died of his second heart attack the year he painted this head. Is it another of his self-portraits? It can be taken as one, but it is the head's ambiguity, its refusal to let on its intentions, that renders the question secondary at best. The head is either part of the way up the hill or part of the way down. It is the image of a life at rest or a life never to be at rest, a life in between, a life that can only look up to . . . to where? What does this unwavering eye see in this barren anywhere?

We will never know, and we may be right in guessing that Guston himself did not know. The head does not seem to depend on what it sees. It is an image of endurance, of having suffered indignities and punishments for its unrestrained looking, looking it persists in regardless of what there is to be seen. Even on this hill's side, especially here, there is a degree of attention that is both willed and beyond willing. This head is, as are so many late Gustons, an oracle. It has wisdom to speak, but we must imagine its words. Is it trying to remember some epigrammatic brilliance of Valéry's about the impossibility of talking about painting? Has it just seen Goya's dog sinking into quicksand? Or is it about to utter the curse that will get it moving again? That it raises so many possibilities, that it is vigilant despite its injuries and in such bleak circumstances is what makes this head indomitable.

Afterword

Jon Imber called with the news of Philip's death. In the days that followed and over that summer, I wrote the poems that made up my elegy for Philip. One incident, I am now reminded, did not make it into these poems.

After Jon's call I walked, my head buzzing with the fact of Philip's death, to the bank to cash a check. There, as I waited in line looking at but not really reading the *New York Times* obituary, one of my old students approached me. He carried a baseball glove into which he pounded his fist. It had been years, he wanted me to remember, since we had seen each other, and now he was "straight," off drugs for good and ready — he pounded the glove — to play ball. He spoke in a loud, excited voice and certainly seemed high to me. I had a half dozen people in front of me and wanted him to go away, but he was eager for my attention. He kept jabbering and pounding his fielder's mitt, and left only after I shook his hand outside the bank.

Now it strikes me that this grotesque boy came from the world of Philip's late paintings. He was as disturbing in his manic intensity as one of Philip's late images, and he also had a comic edge. He was aware that he was acting crazy. The people in line warded him off with laughter that was both nervous and amused. I have not seen him since.

Here are the poems which first appeared in the book *On Blue Note* (Zoland Books, 1989).

Philip Guston 1913-1980

Dear Philip —
The rain, it held off,
for Marni's graduation
that was this afternoon.
Yesterday I wrote you
but you were two days
a dead man, Jon called
this morning to say.
"Oh, no, no" is
this what we always
let out? "Oh, no" and
"At least he . . ."
Well, you did live
to see your show go up
by force of will
your "life" the paper
reports you called it.
It is a triumph
and that's what I wrote
yesterday. To Musa
I write today
of your "ferocious delicacy."

HERB GARDEN

Working by hand
and with pitchfork
or hoe, pulling out
two years' weeds
from the herb garden.
Tenacious witchgrass
and in the oregano
thyme and chives
grass and clover.
The ringing thunk
of a clean driven nail.
New house going up
on an old meadow.
Where the barn was,
nothing. And only a few
blackberry canes left.
Dig and then clear
asparagus plants that came
too early for anyone.
What roots! Wigs,
interconnected wigs
of meaty pipes!
Good to work
up a sweat
feel the dirt

on my hands
wiped across my forehead.
Plant basil, bush
of the small leaf kind,
and flat leaf parsley.
Dill and basil seed.
New French tarragon
plant the old still
here but nearly over–
come by grass is puny.
For a border
DRURY bricks late
of the chimney
orange, brittle, knocked
into place sometimes
come apart in flakes.

POSTSCRIPT

Those asparagus plants
I put in the day
after Gordon Cairnie died
as a memorial
boasting they would
last and yield
for sixty years
so my children
might be around
to pick and eat
them remembering.
In six years but
two thin stalks
the rest went to seed
after the stalks grew
tall beautifully into
lacy arrowhead ferns
so heavy they fell
into sage and chives.
Now it is Philip dead
and in the roots
I grip and tug
caught is a nail
hand forged like
those he painted
common and austere.

A smoking cigar
like a turd, we agreed,
the one you painted
a goodsize healthy turd.
You love a painter
and he dies,
leaves the world
full of his images.
At the framers
they shake their heads
"Sorry to hear . . ."
As am I, as am I
when there on the tar
behind the police station
the cigar tossed
from a cop car
the cop's sneer
still on it
lip wet and smoking still.

Smoke

The clouds are x rays.
A coarse towel
reddens my already
sunburned chest. Good
feeling its roughness
after a swim.
Lake water mumbles
lapping at my feet
a sound measured
and beautiful, comforting
as a child's breathing
in sleep.
Down the beach
near the boathouse
I saw a mink.
It stopped short
when it saw me
spun round and dove
black and sleek.
I sat stunned, excited
too slow to react.
Basil snorts, chomping
a pinecone
he tears up
the pine needle path.
Anemic Queen Anne's lace
has the field with

chocolate crowned
misnamed black-eyed
susans and young gold
and green goldenrod.
Asters about to show
yellow centered round
spoked and spiky flowers
and on into dry
ruddy autumn.
The Cat growls
and blasts, lets up
and through comes
the ring of nails
set and driven.
Arden sleeps on
nursing a strep throat.
Marni went to Montpelier
and Bev in humid
hot Boston swelters
home to an empty house.
On the warm brick steps
blue bowl of crayons
softening in the sun.
More here now Philip
in death hardly a day
passes without one sudden
vision of your powerful
bulky physical being

and white hair parted
so far down on the left.
I will not see again
I saw last in March.
Jon took photographs.
We lit up. "Let's,"
you laughed, "get a little
smoke into this one."

Illustration
Acknowledgments

PHILIP GUSTON'S DRAWINGS

Frontispiece: drawing appeared on the cover of *Fire Exit*, a magazine edited by William Corbett; from the private collection of Ray Kass. p. ii.

Slim Jim, from the private collection of William and Beverly Corbett. p. 9.

Figure in Bed, 1977, from the private collection of William and Beverly Corbett. p. 32.

Drawing of Nixon on a letter to William Corbett, from the private collection of William and Beverly Corbett. p. 50.

The Richard Nixon Story, from the private collection of William and Beverly Corbett. p. 52.

Walker Evans Dead, from the private collection of Michael Palmer and Cathy Simon. p. 69.

Memorial Day, from the private collection of Ben and Judith Watkins. p. 71.

Easter, from the private collection of William and Beverly Corbett. p. 72.

May 14, from the private collection of Stratis Haviaras and Heather Cole. p. 73.

Drawing appeared on the cover of *Columbus Square Journal*, by William Corbett, Angel Hair Books, 1976, from the private collection of William and Beverly Corbett. p. 96.

PHILIP GUSTON'S PAINTINGS

Smoke, (on the cover), (1978), Private Collection, New York; courtesy McKee Gallery, New York.

The Studio (1969), Private Collection, New York; courtesy McKee Gallery.

Painting, Smoking, Eating (1973), Stedelijk Museum, Amsterdam.

Monument (1976), Tate Gallery, London/Art Resource, New York.

Source (1976), Edward R. Broida Trust, Palm Beach, Florida; courtesy McKee Gallery.

Pyramid and Shoe (1977), Private Collection, New York; courtesy McKee Gallery.

Painter's Forms (1972), The Estate of Philip Guston, New York; courtesy McKee Gallery.

117

Bibliography

Ashton, Dore, *Yes, but . . . A Critical Study of Philip Guston*. New York: The Viking Press, 1976, revised edition, Berkeley: University of California Press, 1993.

Babel, Isaac, *The Collected Stories*, edited and translated by Walter Morison, Introduction by Lionel Trilling. New York: Meridan, 1960.

Berger, John, *Keeping the Rendezvous*. New York: Pantheon, 1992.

Berkson, Bill, "Dialogue with Philip Guston," *Art and Literature*, VII, Winter, 1965.

Bunting, Basil, *Collected Poems*, Mt. Kisco: Moyer Bell Limited, 1985.

Feld, Ross, *Philip Guston*. New York: George F. Braziller, 1980.

Feldman, Morton, "Give My Regards to 8th Street," *Morton Feldman Essays*. Germany: Beginner Press, 1985.

Hughes, Robert, *The Shock of the New*, revised edition. New York: Alfred A. Knopf, 1991.

Mayer, Musa, *Night Studio: A Memoir of Philip Guston*. New York: Alfred A. Knopf, 1988.

Paustovsky, Konstantin, "Reminiscences" *Partisan Review*, III-IV, 1961.

Perl, Jed, *Paris Without End*. San Francisco: North Point Press, 1988.

Storr, Robert, *Guston*. New York: Abbeville Modern Masters, 1986.